pearl harbor 1941

the day of infamy

CARL SMITH

pearl harbor 1941

the day of infamy

Praeger Illustrated Military History Series

PRAEGER

Westport, Connecticut
London

Library of Congress Cataloging-in-Publication Data

Smith, Carl, 1946–
  Pearl Harbor 1941: the day of infamy / Carl Smith.
    p. cm – (Praeger illustrated military history, ISSN 1547-206X)
  Originally published: Oxford: Osprey, 1999.
  Includes bibliographical references and index.
  ISBN 0-275-98272-6 (alk. paper)
  1. Pearl Harbor (Hawaii), Attack on, 1941. I. Title. II. Series.
  D767.92.S62   2004
  940.54'26693–dc22 2003063217

British Library Cataloguing in Publication Data is available.

First published in paperback in 1999 by Osprey Publishing Limited, Elms Court,
Chapel Way, Botley, Oxford OX2 9LP. All rights reserved.

Copyright © 2004 by Osprey Publishing Limited

Library of Congress Catalog Card Number: 2003063217
ISBN: 0-275-98272-6
ISSN: 1547-206X

Praeger Publishers, 88 Post Road West, Westport, CT 06881
An imprint of Greenwood Publishing Group, Inc.
www.praeger.com

Printed in China through World Print Ltd.

The paper used in this book complies with the Permanent Paper Standard issued
by the National Information Standards Organization (Z39.48-1984).

10 9 8 7 6 5 4 3 2 1

ILLUSTRATED BY: Jim Laurier

CONTENTS

KEY TO MILITARY SYMBOLS

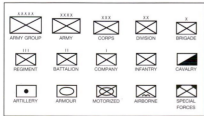

INTRODUCTION

Bored servicemen in Hawaii were always vocal about living conditions or carping about food and barracks life. A Soldier's Prayer was circulated at Hawaiian military installations just prior to the attack. After December 7, boredom was forgotten.

LEFT Pearl was a natural harbor that had been used for over 100 years. An early visitor was the battleship USS *Texas*, shown here with sun awnings in place over the foredeck. In 1940, the Pacific Fleet transferred from California, worrying Japanese military strategists, who saw it as a threat to Japanese security. *Texas* was serving in the Atlantic at the time of the Japanese attack.

Below, thick fluffy clouds blanketed the blue sky. Shoving the stick forward, Lt. Mitsuo Matsuzaki dropped his Kate AI-301 beneath them into more blue sky, the horizon broken by the low verdant land mass he was approaching. His observer, Cmdr Mitsuo Fuchida, the mission commander, was watchful. Hawaii looked green and oddly peaceful. He scanned the horizon. It looked too good to be true; other than his fliers, no planes were visible. Fuchida remembered, years later, how peaceful it had appeared.

It was 0730 hrs Hawaii time; the date, December 7, 1941. Fuchida's destination was the home of the US Pacific Fleet – Pearl Harbor. The fleet and three aircraft carriers berthed there were the key targets. A statement notifying the US that war had been declared had been scheduled for delivery to Washington an hour earlier. This air strike would be the first act of war between Imperial Japan and the United States.

All the planning, endless exercises, and practice runs would determine the success of this attack. Some military minds thought it would cripple the US fleet; others hoped it might scare the Americans into appeasement; but most felt it would pull Japan into a war with the United States. If war was to be the outcome, some had said, then let it begin here, because Japan's best hope for winning a conflict with the Western giant was to strike first and cripple the US Navy. Japanese forces could then act with a free hand in the following months and further expand their conquests. For Cmdr Fuchida much of this was immaterial, for he was a career officer with a mission: bomb Pearl Harbor.

Political background

The Hawaiian Islands lie in the middle of the Pacific, west-south-west of the United States, the first real landfall west of the mainland, positioned at 150°–170° longitude (just east of the International Date Line) and between 18° and 29° north of the equator. Kauai, Niihau, Oahu, Molokai, Maui, Kahoolawe, Lanai, and Hawaii form the major islands in the chain, originally called the Sandwich Islands. The northernmost edge is at roughly the same latitude as Los Angeles, giving the Hawaiian Islands a uniform, mild annual temperature of 75° Fahrenheit and a tropical climate, with cooling ocean breezes, rainforests, and dramatic stretches of beach at the foot of majestic mountains and volcanoes. These islands, between Japan and the United States, are a perfect military base, first for naval attack and then for air power.

Hawaii had been discovered by Europeans in the mid-1700s. First ruled by a monarchy, in 1900 it became a US territory, but it was not made a state until 1959. The land is fertile and the beaches, when properly cultivated, yield immense crops of American, Japanese and

THE JAPANESE GREATER EAST ASIA CO-PROSPERITY SPHERE

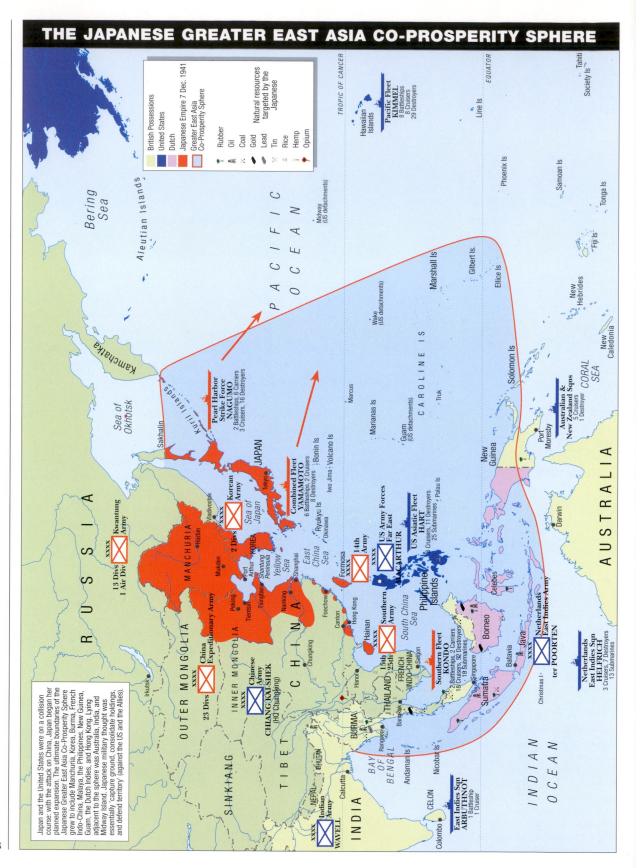

Japan and the United States were on a collision course: with the attack on China, Japan began her planned expansion. The ultimate boundaries of the Japanese Greater East Asia Co-Prosperity Sphere grew to include Manchuria, Korea, Burma, French Indo-China, Malaya, the Philippines, New Guinea, Guam, the Dutch Indies, and Hong Kong. Lying adjacent to the sphere was Australia, India, and Midway Island. Japanese military thought was essentially capture ground, consolidate holdings, and defend territory (against the US and the Allies).

Legend:
- British Possessions
- United States
- Dutch
- Japanese Empire 7 Dec. 1941
- Greater East Asia Co-Prosperity Sphere
- Natural resources targeted by the Japanese
  - Rubber
  - Oil
  - Coal
  - Gold
  - Lead
  - Tin
  - Rice
  - Hemp
  - Opium

Pacific Fleet KIMMEL
8 Battleships
8 Cruisers
29 Destroyers

Pearl Harbor Strike Force NAGUMO
2 Battleships, 6 Carriers
3 Cruisers, 16 Destroyers

Kwantung Army
13 Divs XXXX
1 Air Div

Korean Army
2 Divs XXXX

Combined Fleet YAMAMOTO
6 Battleships, 8 Carriers
8 Cruisers, 2 Cruisers
8 Destroyers

14th Army XXXX

US Army Forces Far East MACARTHUR

US Asiatic Fleet HART
3 Cruisers, 11 Destroyers
25 Submarines

China Expeditionary Army XXXX

Chinese Army XXXX
23 Divs
CHIANG KAI-SHEK
(HQ Chungking)

Southern Army XXXX

15th 25th
THAILAND

Southern Fleet KONDO
2 Battleships, 2 Carriers
18 Cruisers, 50 Destroyers
18 Submarines

Australian & New Zealand Sqns
5 Cruisers
1 Destroyer

Netherlands East Indies Army ter POORTEN XXXX

Netherlands East Indies Sqn HELFRICH
3 Cruisers, 7 Destroyers
13 Submarines

Indian Army XXXX
WAVELL

East Indies Sqn ARBUTHNOT
1 Battleship
1 Cruiser

8

RIGHT **Pearl Harbor was the first stopping point in Pacific waters. Because air power attack was theoretical, Pearl's fortifications relied heavily on coastal guns in heavy positions to defend against naval bombardment.**

Despite the war in Europe, in 1941 the US Army was not ready to fight a "modern" war. Although in 1936-issue field gear, these soldiers on maneuvers would look at home in French trenches a quarter of a century earlier. Note the cloth puttees, campaign hats and gas masks reminiscent of World War I.

international tourists. By the 1930s, the population of Hawaii was mostly American and Asian, with its indigenous peoples waning.

Japan noted the islands as a potential threat to expansion. Since before the Russo-Japanese War, Japan had been full-steam-ahead modernizing, manufacturing and upgrading its military. With these changes came increased demand for natural resources (steel, oil, gas, raw materials and minerals) and their eyes turned east to China, Indochina, and the islands of the Pacific. Although Russia had traditionally been viewed as the major threat to Japanese expansion and Asian influence, the American and European presence in Asia became increasingly important.

The Japanese felt European powers were limiting growth of their empire: as Japan expanded, European resistance coalesced which in turn supported Japanese fears of intervention and limitation. The US Congress placed restrictions on business with Japan, and then the majority of the US Pacific Fleet made Pearl Harbor its home. Real or imagined, the US fleet posed a threat, and Japan viewed Hawaii with special interest.

The situation worsened as Japan felt strangled and besieged. When war erupted in Europe, and the United States did not intervene as France and Britain became embroiled in conflict with Germany and Italy, Japan noticed. America, it seemed, wanted neutrality: perhaps they would overlook expansions in Asia.

Europeans might have to fight wars on two fronts, but obviously Europe would be their primary theater and the Pacific would occupy a back seat. The US Pacific Fleet was a deterrent. Japanese and American spheres of influence grew, stretching thinner, threatening to burst. Japan and the United States moved on a collision course: the former needed to grow, the latter wanted to maintain the status quo. Relations worsened, and nationalistic distrust blossomed.

On December 7, 1941, at 0750 hrs, the situation exploded. Within hours, the United States was no longer neutral.

OPPOSING COMMANDERS

Admiral Husband E. Kimmel

Admiral Husband (Hubby) E. Kimmel (1882–1968) was the naval commander at Pearl Harbor in 1941. Born in Henderson, Kentucky, the son of an army major, he graduated from the Naval Academy in 1904. In February, 1941, he was promoted over 32 other officers to Commander in Chief Pacific (CinCPAC), becoming the navy's senior admiral. Admiral Stark, Chief of Naval Operations (CNO) in Washington, had every confidence in Kimmel's abilities.

As CinCPAC, Kimmel moved to Pearl Harbor, home of the Pacific Fleet. Gen. Marshall advised Gen. Short that Kimmel was reasonable and responded well to "plain speaking." Kimmel was unhappy with the defense arrangements in Hawaii and at Pearl Harbor. Responsibility for them was split: the army was responsible for land and air defense; the navy for the Navy Yard itself. The navy was responsible for reconnaissance but the army controlled the radar stations and both air and shore defenses in case of invasion. Kimmel let his strong feelings about the tangled web of responsibilities be known.

The US military was understrength and complacent, behind in naval air power and Army Air Corps aircraft, and still thinking of the last war. Weapons, ammunition, and manpower were available, but the overriding mentality was that supplies were to be preserved rather than consumed. Kimmel complained to Washington about inequities.

Without supplies and material, service personnel could not do an adequate job. On top of this, the army and navy competed for allocations, and each had its own "turf" to protect. There was no open rivalry, but clearly the army did not wish to step on the navy's toes and vice-versa, so Kimmel and Short co-operated; but within that inter-service co-operation there was competition and a general lack of sharing any overlapping information. Kimmel was friendly with Short, but each man ran his own show.

Kimmel resented the US policy of building up the Atlantic Fleet at the expense of the Pacific Fleet.

Admiral Kimmel (center) and two members of his staff, his operations officer, Cpt. Delaney (left), and his assistant chief of staff, Cpt. Smith (right). Although aggressive and vigilant, Kimmel shared responsibility for Pearl Harbor with Gen. Short. Both were surprised by the audacious Japanese thrust at an island almost everyone thought too well defended to be a target.

American artillery units on Oahu regularly deployed for field maneuvers and war games. Although a strong fortress, many felt the real threat to Oahu was naval bombardment followed by invasion, rather than air attack.

Schofield Barracks was the main US Army barracks at Pearl Harbor. Security was not in full force until after the Japanese attack. Note the guardhouses to either side of a swing gate bearing the legend "Closed."

The US Navy was a deterrent, but transferring ships and men from the Pacific to the Atlantic affected more than his command – it affected the security of the United States. Still, he was a career officer, and having stated his objections, he followed orders.

Following the events at Pearl Harbor, eight separate investigations of the attack were carried out. Kimmel retired in March, 1942, but went to work as a consultant for a government contractor on secret naval projects. The outraged American public, however, reasoned that someone had to be at fault, and Kimmel and Short were, at the least, censured for failing to coordinate and cooperate better in the defense of Hawaii. They had been in command when the Japanese struck, and in the minds of many members of the American public, they were responsible.

There is a two-year statute of limitations on courts martial, and both Kimmel and Short requested one to clear their names, offering to waive the two-year limitation. A court martial before the end of the war was out of the question, partly because of the difficulty of bringing all witnesses together, and partly because of the desire to keep secret the fact that the US had broken the MAGIC code.

Kimmel rightly felt he had been made a scapegoat, and in the end the Pearl Harbor investigations revealed that if Kimmel was guilty of anything, it was only of an error of judgment, for which many others in higher positions could similarly be censured. To many, however, Kimmel was guilty until proven innocent. At first he looked forward to the prospect of a court martial because, he declared, information had been withheld from him which would prove a mitigating circumstance. As time progressed, however, he became bitter and felt betrayed, and when Forrestal finally offered him a court martial in August, 1945, he declined, preferring to wait until the Congressional investigation was completed. The final report stated that he was guilty of an error of judgment but not of dereliction of duty. The source of blame was to be found in Washington and Hawaii. Kimmel felt vindicated, but he was unhappy that

this had taken several years. He died on May 14, 1968, in Groton, Connecticut.

Major-General Walter C. Short

Major-General Walter C. Short (1880–1949) was the army commander at Pearl Harbor. Born on March 30, 1880, in Fillmore, Illinois, a doctor's son, he graduated from the University of Illinois and accepted a commission in 1901. A training officer in France in World War One, he later went to Fort Benning as assistant commandant and was promoted to brigadier-general in 1936. He was given command of 1st Infantry Division and, at the outbreak of World War Two, that of 1st Corps. On February 8, 1941, he was promoted to lieutenant-general and given command of the Hawaiian Department.

Short was quiet, dignified and an able organizer. His men were well drilled but, under his command, unit commanders carefully watched the use of expendable ammunition and materiel. Short followed his orders to the letter, but failed to read between the lines. He was surprised when the Japanese attacked Pearl Harbor. Ten days after the attack, he was recalled to Washington and replaced by Gen. Emmons. An army investigation found Short derelict in properly directing his staff. The general was quiet, believing that a court martial after hostilities were over, and when a full disclosure could be made, would vindicate him.

He reverted to his permanent rank of major-general and retired at the end of February, 1942. He accepted the position of traffic manager at the Dallas Ford plant, which made cars and war goods. Although he maintained a low public profile and did not speak with outsiders, he wanted vindication. During the final investigation Short declared that he had not been given adequate warning from Washington and had been suffering from a lack of resources. The investigation revealed that both Washington and Hawaiian commanders had been at fault. Short requested a court martial but never received one. He died on September 3, 1949 in Dallas.

Admiral Harold R. Stark

Harold (Betty) R. Stark was born on November 12, 1880, in Wilkes-Barre, Pennsylvania, and graduated from Annapolis in 1903. He was befriended by Franklin Delano Roosevelt (FDR) and was awarded the DSM in World War One.

In 1939, Stark became Chief of Naval Operations (CNO) and overcame strong isolationist sentiment to start construction of modern naval vessels and bases. He beefed up the Pacific Fleet at Pearl, and aided by information from the MAGIC code, knew that Japanese–American relations were drastically declining and approaching a state of war. He gave commanders warnings, but because of the belief that Pearl Harbor was too strong, he felt the Japanese would attack elsewhere. When Nomura's message was translated by MAGIC on December 7, 1941, he started to send a message to Pearl Harbor, but Marshall assured him that army communications could get it there just as fast. It

In the 1930s, the "special tractor" light tank was typical of US materiel. It was modeled after the Renault tank and bore too many angled surfaces that would trap shellfire rather than deflect it. Note the heavy plates instead of treads, which were adopted later.

arrived after the air raid had begun. Stark was relieved as CNO on March 7, 1942, but Marshall was not removed.

On October 1, 1943, Stark took over command of the 12th Fleet to prepare US Naval Forces for the Normandy invasion; he was liaison with the Admiralty and Churchill. He testified in the Pearl Harbor hearings and retired on April 1, 1946. He died on August 20, 1972, at his home in Washington, DC.

General George C. Marshall

A Kentuckian whose lineage could be traced back to the American Revolution, George C. Marshall was born on December 31, 1880, in Allentown. Promoted to lieutenant-colonel, he went to France with the AEF, becoming head of operations and training for the 1st Army. He refurbished the army's officer training regiment, implemented Roosevelt's "CCC" program through the military in the southern states, and was promoted to chief of war plans and finally deputy to the army's chief of staff.

FDR appointed Marshall as chief of staff on September 1, 1939, and gave him his fourth star. Marshall supported the concept of an independent army air corps, and some feel he neglected other branches, building up this new branch at their expense. He was chief of staff when the Japanese attacked Pearl Harbor, but unlike many others, no stigma for the debacle was attached to him.

Marshall fully supported the "defeat Germany first" concept, and many blame the length of the Pacific War on his cautious approach to planning and implementation of war plans. After the war, he became Secretary of State, and he is primarily remembered as the author of the Marshall Plan that reinvigorated Europe. He was awarded the Nobel Peace Prize and died on October 16, 1959.

Cordell Hull

Lanky and tall, born in a log cabin in Tennessee on October 2, 1871, by his twentieth birthday Cordell Hull had become a circuit judge, through his hard work and diligence.

In 1933, he became Secretary of State under FDR. He and Roosevelt became close friends, and although Roosevelt acted as his own secretary of state on most occasions, Hull was a good subordinate and had great

President Franklin Delano Roosevelt had already agreed with Britain that the US would abide by a "defeat Germany first" policy if the US entered the war. The attack on Pearl Harbor would test American resolve.

influence in matters of foreign policy.

Hull met with Nomura on December 7, 1941: although he probably did believe that the Japanese ambassador had been unaware of the 14-part message until too late, Hull read Nomura the riot act, soundly denouncing the Japanese attack after he had received word of it via chain of command.

Hull tendered his resignation November 21, 1944. He was awarded the Nobel Peace Prize in 1945 and died in 1955.

President Franklin Delano Roosevelt

Roosevelt, known simply as FDR, is the only American president to have served four consecutive terms, from 1933 until his death in 1945. A distant cousin of Teddy Roosevelt, he graduated from Harvard without distinction. In 1910, he was appointed Secretary of the Navy. In August, 1921, while on holiday at Campobello, he was struck with polio, which left him crippled from the waist down, though he later regained partial use of his legs.

In 1928, Roosevelt was elected governor of New York: four years later he was elected to his first four-year term as president. He established the New Deal conglomerate of economic legislation, designed to help the struggling American economy, and in so doing made himself the champion of the little man.

Although America remained neutral when war broke out in Europe, Roosevelt noted, in a fireside chat on September 1, 1939, that he could not ask all Americans to remain neutral in thought. When Pearl Harbor was bombed, he denounced the action in a speech that decried December 7 as a "day that will live in infamy."

He piloted the US through the darkest days of World War Two, but it was too much for him, and he died on April 12, 1945, at Warm Springs, Georgia. His imprint on American political thought remains visible to this day.

Admiral Isoroku Yamamoto

The seventh son of a schoolteacher, Yamamoto was born April 4, 1884. Isoroku means "56," which was his father's age when he was born. He lived near Nagaoka, entered naval school at 16, and graduated as seventh in his class. He was an ensign on a cruiser in the Battle of Tsushima in the Russo-Japanese War in 1905, when he lost two fingers on his left hand. He was adopted by the Yamamoto family and took their name. Yamamoto was promoted to commander and transferred to Tokyo naval headquarters, where he married: however, he was sent to Harvard to study economics, and also learned about petroleum. While World War One raged, he discovered the military use of aviation. He was fond of playing *go* and *shogi*, and was a guest at many dinner parties, also learning poker and bridge.

In 1923, Cpt. Yamamoto was head of the air training base at Kasumigaura and became naval attaché to Washington. At the London naval conference, he convinced all that the 5:5:3 ratio was no longer acceptable, and it was discarded. He returned to Japan as a diplomatic hero and became Vice-Minister of the Navy.

Yamamoto favored air power, and he relegated the steel navy to a secondary position, opposing the building of the battleships *Yamato* and

Fleet Admiral Isoroku Yamamoto was Japan's leading proponent of naval air power and did not wish a prolonged war with the US. He felt Japan could not win, but once Japan entered it, he fought hard for his homeland. Yamamoto was the force behind the Hawaii Operation.

Musashi as antiquated technology, saying: "These … will be as useful … as a samurai sword." He championed new aircraft carriers, opposed Japan's entry into the Tripartite Pact in 1939, opposed the war hawks, and acknowledged that although he could run wild for six months to a year, after that time he had no confidence whatever in Japan's ability to win a naval war.

In mid-August, 1939, he was promoted to full admiral and became commander-in-chief of the Combined Fleet. He became a Rommel-like figure to the men of his command, inspiring them to greater efforts by his confidence, and improved the combat readiness and seaworthiness of the Japanese Navy by making it practice in good and bad weather, day and night.

Yamamoto did not wish to go to war with the US, but once the government had decided, he devoted himself to the task of giving Japan the decisive edge. He decided that Pearl Harbor would be won with air power, not battleships. The plan to attack Pearl Harbor was his.

After the success at Pearl Harbor, Yamamoto suffered a defeat at Midway: this has been likened to Lee's early success at Chancellorsville followed by his defeat at Gettysburg. Some have speculated that he was overconfident. During the battle for Guadalcanal, he decided to visit his men to inspire confidence and improve morale. His plane was shot down on April 18, 1943, by American fighters.

His death deprived the Japanese military not only of a courageous and insightful leader, but also of a man who was a true military professional, a man who fought but wanted peace. Had he lived, the outcome of the war would probably not have changed: however, his stature and efforts might have shortened the struggle.

Commander Mitsuo Fuchida

Born in Nara Prefecture on December 2, 1902, in the Year of the Tiger, Mitsuo Fuchida was clever, outspoken, and personally fearless. In 1921,

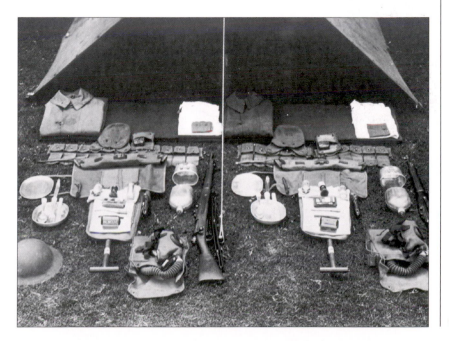

In early 1941, army issue equipment was far behind where it would be a scant five years later. Bolt-action Springfields, old gas masks, and "dishpan" helmets would shortly be replaced when war production went into high gear.

he entered the Naval Academy and shortly thereafter befriended Minoru Genda when they discovered a shared love for flying. Their friendship and mutual respect was to last for years, and in many ways it helped shape the concept of air war and the attack on Pearl Harbor. Somewhat ironically, he once characterized his friend Genda as "reckless."

First specializing in horizontal bombing, Fuchida gained such prowess that he was made an instructor. Shortly thereafter, he was promoted to lieutenant-commander and was accepted into the Naval Staff College. It was there that he espoused naval air power.

In 1939 he joined the *Akagi* as flight commander. On sea exercises he met Adm. Yamamoto, who expressed his real interest in naval aviation. Fuchida came to respect Yamamoto and became a devoted supporter of the admiral. After a short stint on *Ryuho*, he returned to the *Akagi* with more than 3,000 hours of flight time under his wings. While in China, he learned the art of torpedo bombing, and was recognized throughout the IJN as a torpedo ace.

Fuchida was a hard-headed officer who tenaciously defended an idea until it was proven untenable; then he compromised. He had a sly sense of humor, defended the underdog, and was a kind, gentle man in private life, but he had the spirit of a warrior. Nicknamed "Buddha" by his friends for his good humor, he was an officer who planned things down to the last detail, had insight into tactical and strategic situations, and was personally brave and respected by his men. Genda once said of him:

"He was … our best flight leader … with a clear head. The success of the Pearl Harbor attack depended upon the character and ability of its flight leader, and that is why … Fuchida was selected for the job."

He coordinated all preparations for the attack on Pearl Harbor and personally led the first wave, flying as an observer with Lt. Mitsuo Matsuzaki. He wanted to conduct a second attack against Pearl Harbor, but Nagumo decided they had done well enough and turned the task force home.

Fuchida met the Emperor face to face and provided details of the assault on Pearl Harbor: later he said it was easier to go into combat than to face him then. Sidelined at Midway by appendicitis, Fuchida was soon back on duty and was active throughout the remainder of the war. Afterwards, he converted to Christianity, became a minister, and wrote about the Pearl Harbor attack. He died in 1976.

Commander Minoru Genda

Born in 1904, Genda attended the naval training school and shortly afterwards met Mitsuo Fuchida. Genda served in the oldest Japanese fighter squadron, the Yokosuka Air Group, under Lt. Kobayashi. Their aerial acrobatics quickly gained the group the sobriquet "Genda's Circus." He was recognized as a superior fighter pilot and air operations officer.

Rear Admiral Onishi had Genda write a feasibility study for a proposed Japanese attack on Pearl Harbor. Commander Genda wrote the study and constructed a strategy with ten main points, most of which were incorporated into the final plan. He developed the First Air Group's torpedo program, and proposed a second attack on Pearl Harbor several days after the first, wanting to annihilate the US fleet. He remained aboard *Akagi* as Nagumo's air advisor, and was on deck to welcome Fuchida's flight back.

In 1941, artillery units on maneuvers (shown here with unit's terrier mascot) deployed and entrenched using camouflage, in the belief that some day they might have to fight off naval invaders.

Sunday morning on December 7, 1941, at Ford Island would have looked as peaceful as this shot, taken barely four weeks earlier. Note *Lexington* (CV2) on the west side of the island (top of picture) and Battleship Row on the east side (bottom of picture). Japanese intelligence regularly scoured newspapers for word of naval comings and goings.

Genda was important in the Midway attacks, taking Fuchida's place in the squadron since the latter was recuperating following his operation. Later he was promoted to captain and posted as senior officer in charge of naval aviation on the general staff. When Air Group 343 formed in December, 1944, Genda transferred from general staff to become its commander. He stressed formation combat, improved air-to-air communications, and advance intelligence of enemy air formations. He led the group in the Battle of Okinawa, and commanded Air Group 343 until the end of the war.

Vice-Admiral Chuichi Nagumo

Chuichi Nagumo was born in 1887. Of fiery temperament, this career naval officer was an expert in torpedo warfare. His military stratagems were often aggressive but uninspired and sometimes ill-advised.

Vice-Admiral Nagumo was appointed commander of Kido Butai, the 1st Air Fleet, despite his lack of familiarity and experience in naval aviation. He commanded the 1st Air Fleet at Pearl Harbor from the deck of his flagship, *Akagi*. Two attack waves were planned, and results indicated a third strike would not yield any further success. The Americans were now somewhat prepared and would probably have inflicted disproportionate casualties on the attack force. Subsequent events have shown that attacking harbor facilities probably would have further crippled US ability to strike back.

Afterwards, he led the 1st Air Fleet in the Dutch East Indies, the Indian Ocean and at Midway, where he lost *Akagi, Kaga, Hiryu* and *Soryu*, four of Japan's finest carriers, because of poor tactical ability and bad luck. The magnitude of this loss disconcerted him, and he lost his drive and any effectiveness he possessed as a commander. As a subordinate of Adm. Kondo, he helped achieve the Japanese tactical victory (but strategic defeat) at Santa Cruz.

At Saipan in 1944, he commanded a backwater fleet of barges, patrol boats and infantry. When the inevitable result of the war became clear, he committed suicide, on July 6, 1944.

Ambassador Kichisaburo Nomura

Admiral Kichisaburo Nomura was the Japanese ambassador to Washington at the time of Pearl Harbor, and was cast unwittingly in the role of villain.

Born in 1877, he was orphaned, and later adopted by Masatane Nomura, taking his name. In 1898, he graduated from the Naval Academy with imperial honors for scholarship. He commanded the 3rd Fleet during the 1932 Shanghai Incident, coming through the conflict unscathed, only to lose his left eye to a terrorist bomb just weeks afterwards.

Nomura retired from active duty but served as foreign minister in the government from September 23, 1939, to January 14, 1940. His was a voice of constraint and caution, encouraging diplomatic solutions.

In February, 1941, Nomura was sent to the United States as ambassador to Washington. As he opposed Japanese militarists, he was welcomed and trusted when he tried to reconcile US–Japanese differences with Cordell Hull.

Both Hirohito and Yamamoto insisted that at least 30 minutes notice be given the US prior to the outbreak of hostilities at Pearl Harbor. A message was sent to Nomura: he was to give it to Hull at one o'clock Washington time. The message was sent in 14 parts and decoded as it arrived. Because of the security on this message, Nomura did not have a competent typist with sufficient clearance. The person selected was slow and Nomura postponed his appointment until 1400 hrs. However, the US had broken the code, but was confused about the intent of the message because it neither declared war nor offered hope of peace through further negotiations.

Nomura saw Hull at 1420 and delivered the message. Hull was infuriated and terse during the meeting. Nomura soon found the reason for Hull's reception: Pearl Harbor had been attacked by Japan. Hull declared to the press immediately afterwards that he had never seen a message so full of "falsehoods and distortions … on a scale so huge that I never imagined … any government … was capable of uttering them." Nomura was shaken by the revelation that Japan had attacked the US and, shoulders sagging, he left Hull's office.

Nomura and his staff were interned, and remained so until 1942, when he was repatriated. After the war he became president of the Japan Victor Company and was a member of the House of Councilors. He died in 1964.

CHRONOLOGY

1936

December 2 - Yamamoto begins forging the naval air arm into a modern weapon.

1939

February 10 - Japan occupies the Chinese island of Hainan.

August - Adm. Isoroku Yamamoto appointed commander-in-chief of the Imperial Japanese Navy.

September 4 - Yamamoto writes to V/Adm. Shimata to say that he is uneasy about "Japan's relations with Germany and Italy in the face of changes now taking place in Europe."

1940

Spring - The US fleet transfers to Pearl Harbor as its permanent home base: to the Japanese, this is a thinly veiled threat. Yamamoto uses this to urge expansion of naval air power. Yamamoto begins thinking that it would be better to carry war to the US Navy rather than wait for them to choose the time and place for battle.

July - Roosevelt has an embargo placed on all aviation fuel, steel and scrap iron to Japan.

August - Lieutenant-Colonel Friedman, a cryptographer, breaks the Japanese Purple Code (MAGIC).

September 3 - Roosevelt gives Britain 50 old destroyers for the right to establish US naval bases in British territories.

September 4 - The US warns Japan not to attack French Indochina.

September 11 - Ojiro Okuda is appointed acting consul general to Hawaii. He is in charge of reporting on movements of US ships in the harbor, much of which appears in American newspapers. Kohichi Seki studies Jane's Fighting Ships and travels around the island studying the base and airfields, but without trespassing on US government property though.

September 27 - Japan joins the Tripartite Pact. Yamamoto tells Konoye: "I hope you will … avoid a Japanese–American war."

November 12 - British torpedo bombers attack the Italian fleet at Taranto, disabling half of Italy's Mediterranean fleet.

View of Southeast Loch, looking north from the Hickam Field side, where sub pens and PT berths were located (to right). Battleship Row is out of sight to the left. Mountains, destroyer berths, and Pearl City are faintly visible in the background.

December 10 - Yamamoto writes to Shimada: "The probability is great … our operations against the Netherlands' Indies are almost certain to develop into a war with America, Britain and Holland before those operations are half-over. Consequently we should not launch … the southern operation unless we are prepared … and adequately equipped."

December 30 - Rear Admiral Bloch sends a memo: "Any aircraft attacking Pearl Harbor will … be brought by carriers."

1941

January 1 - In Japan, American ambassador Grew writes in his diary: "Japan … is on the warpath … If … Americans … could read … articles by leading Japanese … they … would realize the utter hopelessness of a policy of appeasement."

January 6 - President Roosevelt declares the United States the "arsenal of democracy."

January 7 - Yamamoto writes a letter to R/Adm. Takijiru Oikawa, saying: "A conflict with the United States … is inevitable." The Japanese Navy should "destroy the US main fleet at the outset of the war." He continues that the Japanese Navy should strike so as to "decide the fate of the war on the very first day." His plan is to find the US Navy "at Pearl Harbor [and] attack it vigorously with our air force." He concludes that if the US Navy is not at Pearl Harbor, they should find them regardless of where they are. The Japanese First and Second Carrier Divisions should mount a "surprise attack with all their air strength, risking themselves on a moonlight night or at dawn." Oilers were needed for refueling at sea, destroyers would pick up survivors whose aircraft or ships went down, and submarines would attack vessels fleeing Pearl Harbor and attempt to sink Allied vessels at the entrance and block it. An attack on "the Philippines and Singapore should be made at almost the same time as … against Hawaii." At the end of the letter, Yamamoto requests: "I sincerely desire to … personally command that attack force."

January 24 - Prince Fumimaro Konoye, the Japanese prime minister, asserts that "firm establishment of a Mutual Prosperity Sphere in Greater East Asia is … necessary to the continued existence of this country." Yamamoto hypothesizes that should war break out "between Japan and the United States, it would not be enough that we take Guam and the Philippines, nor even Hawaii and San Francisco. We would have to … dictate the terms of peace in the White House. I wonder if our politicians … are prepared to make the necessary sacrifices."

January 27 - In secret talks with Britain, the US decides that if Japan enters the war on the German side, and if the US enters the war, Germany is to be defeated first, then Japan. Ambassador Grew, in Japan, is warned by his Peruvian counterpart that he has heard a Japanese worker in his embassy say that if war occurs the "Japanese military … [will] attempt a surprise mass attack on Pearl Harbor using all their military facilities." In Washington, military intelligence is surprised only that Grew puts credence in the source of the report and not in the supposition of the report. In Japan, Foreign Minister Yosuke Matsuoka says, "We must control the Western Pacific," and that the US should reconsider their prior actions: if the US does not, there is "no hope for Japanese–American relations." Aboard *Nagato*, Yamamoto discusses the logical and technical feasibility of an attack on Pearl Harbor. After this meeting, Onishi asks Maeda (his senior staff officer) the following question: if US capital ships were "moored around Ford Island, could a successful torpedo attack be launched against them?" Maeda says no, the water is too shallow for torpedoes to be effective. However, if the torpedoes were modified…

February 1 - Kimmel replaces Richardson as CinCPAC; Short is promoted to commander of the Hawaiian Department.

February 5 - Kimmel receives a letter from Secretary Knox stating: "If war eventuates with Japan … hostilities … would start … with a surprise attack on Pearl Harbor." The letter tells Kimmel to "increase the joint readiness of the army and navy to withstand a raid." He says that probable forms of attack are bombing, torpedo attacks, or both. Congressman Faddis of Pennsylvania states: "The Japanese are not going to risk a fight … where they must face the American Navy in open battle. Their navy is not strong enough."

February 12 - Nomura presents his credentials, which appoint him Ambassador to Washington, to Cordell Hull.

February 15 - Kimmel issues a Pacific Fleet Conference letter saying they are faced with a possible surprise attack on ships in Pearl Harbor.

Mid-February - Onishi sends for Cmdr Minoru Genda and presents Yamamoto's plan, mentioning that Yamamoto has given some thought to making it a one-way mission (*katamechi kogami*) to increase the striking distance to over 500 miles. Genda opposes treating aircraft as disposable: "Ditching … would be a waste of men and planes." He thinks Yamamoto should include dive-bombers and high altitude bombers as well as torpedo planes in the attack. "To obtain the best results, all carriers should approach as close to Pearl Harbor as possible." His last point is: "Our prime target should be US carriers." Onishi asks Genda to prepare a report about feasibility, component forces and manner of execution, and then report back in ten days.

Late February - Genda gives Onishi a report containing ten main proposals. It must be a surprise attack; US carriers are its main objective; US aircraft on Oahu are an objective; and every available Japanese carrier should take part in the operation. Furthermore, all kinds of attack aircraft should be used, and Japanese fighters should play an active role in the attack; the attack should be in early morning; refueling vessels at sea is necessary for success; and all planning must be ultra-secret. The tenth proposal is for a full-scale invasion, which Onishi disagrees with because they could not maintain supply so far from their present bases. Yamamoto wants to cripple the US Navy whereas Genda feels they should annihilate it.

February 27 - Okuda reports: "The fleet goes to sea for a week and stays in Pearl Harbor for one week. Every Wednesday those at sea and those in the harbor change places."

March 5 - The Japanese foreign ministry wires Nomura to say that they feel fairly certain that the US "is reading your code messages."

March 10 - Onishi gives Yamamoto a draft of his plan for attack, based on Genda's plan but with some modifications.

March 11–12 - Congress passes the Lend Lease Act, which supplies materiel to governments fighting the Axis.

March 14 - Kita is appointed consul general to Hawaii.

March 20 - Nomura responds to the foreign ministry: "Though I do not know which ones, I have discovered that the United States is reading some of our codes." Nomura informs them he will tell them details in a "safe" way. Still they did not change the Purple Code. Matsuoka may have been suspicious of Nomura's warning, feeling it sprang from insecurity.

March 27 - Takeo Yoshikawa, an intelligence officer, arrives in Pearl Harbor and realizes that battleships are berthed in pairs and that the in-shore ship is protected from torpedo attacks by the outboard one.

March 30 - Roosevelt orders the Coast Guard to seize two German, 28 Italian and 35 Danish ships in US ports.

April 1 - Naval Intelligence in Washington alerts district commanders to the fact that "the

At the time of the attack on Pearl Harbor, the Army Air Force still had some old and obsolete aircraft such as this twin-engine Dolphin amphibian.

Axis Powers often … [attack on] Saturday and Sunday or on national holidays" and that commanders should put "proper watches and precautions … in effect."

April 10 - The IJN reorganizes into the 1st Air Fleet, consisting of the First Carrier Division (*Kaga* and *Akagi* and four destroyers), the Second Carrier Division (*Hiryu* and *Soryu* and four destroyers) and the Fourth Carrier Division (*Ryuho* and two destroyers).

April 13 - Japan and Russia sign a neutrality pact giving Japan the green light for southward expansion.

April 15 - The US begins shipping lend-lease goods to China.

April 21 - US, English, and Dutch officers coordinate the proposed roles of each in the military defense against Japan in case of a Japanese attack on Singapore.

April 23 - Marshall disagrees with Roosevelt's decision to keep the US fleet in Hawaii because "our heavy bombers and … pursuit planes … could put up such a defense that the Japs wouldn't dare attack Hawaii."

April 28 - When queried about the US choice to strengthen the Atlantic Fleet by removing vessels from the Pacific, the British reply that the "reduction … would not unduly encourage Japan." *New Mexico*, *Mississippi*, *Idaho*, *Yorktown*, four light cruisers, 17 destroyers, three oilers, three transports, and ten auxiliaries are transferred by the end of summer.

May 20 - Nomura confirms to Tokyo: "the US is reading some of our codes."

May 26 - Yoshikawa reports that three battleships and three light cruisers have disappeared from Pearl Harbor. Kimmel fires off an 11-page memo noting that 72 percent of the new officers for the Atlantic came from the Pacific Fleet and that the Pacific Fleet's needs are subordinated to those of Britain and the Atlantic Fleet.

May 27 - Roosevelt declares the US to be in an unlimited state of national emergency.

June 14 - The US freezes German and Italian assets.

June 16 - German consulates in the US are shut down.

June 17 - Germany moves against US property in Germany.

June 20 - The US stops oil shipments from Gulf and East Coast ports to all destinations except Latin America and Britain.

June 22 - Italian consulates in the US are closed.

June 26 - Vichy France permits Japan to occupy French Indochina. The US impounds Japanese credits in the US. Roosevelt nationalizes the Philippine Army.

July 17 - A new Japanese government is formed.

July 28 - The US puts an embargo on oil sales, freezes assets, and closes ports to Japanese vessels.

August 18 - An amendment to the 1940 Selective Service Law extends the length of service for US inductees from one year to two-and-a-half years.

September 24 - A message from Tokyo to the Consulate General instructs the spy to report on US vessels in Pearl Harbor.

October 16 - Konoye resigns and Gen. Tojo sets up a new government with himself as prime minister. Stark warns Kimmel of the possibility of Japanese activities.

November 5 - Yamamoto issues Top Secret Order No.1 to the Combined Fleet, detailing the plan for the attack on Pearl Harbor.

November 7 - Congress repeals sections of the Neutrality Act concerning arming US cargo ships and transporting war goods to warring nations.

November 10 - Britain states that should Japan go to war with the US, they will declare war on Japan "within the hour."

November 22 - The US intercepts a message telling Nomura that the deadline of November 22 has been extended to November 25, 1941.

November 25 - No US–Japanese agreement is reached: consequently, Nagumo's task force sails from the Kuriles.

November 27 - Argentina decides not to sell tungsten to Japan. Kimmel and Short are advised that US–Japanese negotiations have failed and that they should be prepared for any eventuality. Kimmel is ordered to deliver 25 aircraft to Wake and Midway.

December 2 - Nagumo gets the go-ahead. The US intercepts a message to the Japanese Embassy to destroy all codes.

December 6 - Roosevelt is given the partly deciphered 14-part message. Instructions state it is not to be given to Hull until 1300 hrs Washington time on December 7.

December 7 - The Japanese Navy attacks Pearl Harbor.

December 8 - Roosevelt calls the attack on Pearl Harbor a day that will "live in infamy," and Congress declares war on Japan. Gen. Yamashita's 25th Army lands near the borders of Thailand and Malaya and begins the battle for Singapore.

December 11 - Italy and Germany declare war on the US.

December 12 - Japanese forces occupy Guam.

December 23 - Japanese forces capture Wake Island.

December 25 - Hong Kong falls to the Japanese.

1942

February 15 - Singapore surrenders.

THE JAPANESE PLAN

Japan expanded into Asia. US–Japanese relations declined and an embargo on Japanese products sent diplomatic efforts spiraling downward. Ambassador Nomura was appointed and officials hoped he could mend a brittle friendship.

The Japanese government favored controlling Asia's natural resources in what was known as the Southern Resource Area. Japan's treaty with Russia protected her from advances on that front: she already controlled Manchuria, Korea, the eastern third of Mongolia, Shanghai, Formosa, and French Indochina by mid-1941; and now Europe was unable to interfere effectively. The area under Japanese control was called the Greater East Asia Co-Prosperity Sphere. Gen. Hideki Tojo formed a new government in October 1941, with himself as prime minister and the military (primarily the army) under his control.

Ambassador Nomura met repeatedly with Cordell Hull in attempts to reach a solution. Japan would settle for nothing less than the Co-Prosperity Sphere, and negotiations slowed to a standstill. Although neutral, the US thwarted every Japanese attempt to extend Asian influence. With hawks controlling the Japanese government, perhaps Japan could negotiate with the US, but if not, then they would start a blitzkrieg, and when things settled down, they would control the territories they wanted. With European powers occupied, war in Asia would be an unwelcome second front. Nomura had a deadline for diplomatic success that was also the deadline for commencement of a Pacific offensive. Japanese contingency plans would kick in if negotiations with the United States collapsed. The Japanese watched the expansion of Pearl Harbor with considerable interest and concern.

The Japanese hoped to catch the US carriers *Lexington*, *Saratoga* and *Enterprise* at Pearl Harbor. *Saratoga* was at San Diego, *Enterprise* was delivering planes to Wake, and *Lexington* to Midway when the Japanese struck.

The Japanese attack was well planned and the targets plotted. A copy of this contemporary map was captured from a Japanese two-man sub and a Zero fighter. Note the chart is in English, the notations Japanese.

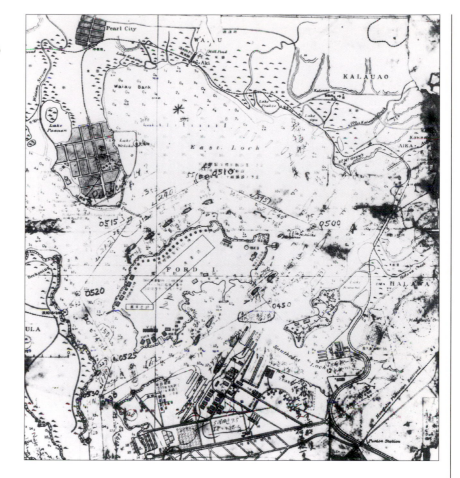

The Japanese held a theory of the "Great All-Out War" with the US Navy. The roots of this near-mythical theory lay in their great victories of Port Arthur and Tsushima, where the Japanese Navy had defeated the Russian fleet. According to the theory, warships led by battleships would steam towards one another in a sea battle the like of which had not been seen since Trafalgar. Japanese warships had been thoughtfully designed to better their American counterparts either with an extra gun, extra speed, more torpedo tubes or anything else which gave each vessel an edge on its opposing number. The Japanese Navy trained under the notion that America was the biggest threat they faced, and that when the smoke of battle drifted away, the Rising Sun would be victorious.

Within the Japanese Navy, there was a rift between the battleship admirals and the younger air power admirals: the former held true to the Great All-Out War theory, while the latter realized that British success at Taranto presaged the future of naval warfare. Yamamoto trained young officers of the Japanese Navy for air war.

In early 1941, Yamamoto began preparation for the Southern Operation, the Japanese plan to conquer the resource-rich areas of Asia. One of the operation's components, the Hawaii Operation, comprised the thrust on Pearl Harbor. Plans were clear: if negotiations had not succeeded by November 23, 1941, a military solution would commence. A code using weather forecast terms was devised and legations were

Smaller destroyers and vessels could moor dockside, such as this visiting German destroyer to Honolulu Harbor in the late 1930s (making the ships and dockside structures "two-for-one" targets for attacking aircraft). Larger vessels had to moor in the naval basin and ferry supplies and personnel abroad by lighter or launches, while garbage scows off-loaded their litter. When mooring dockside, they ran power lines to shore and often shut down their boilers so only minimal power was available: this delayed American vessels from getting immediately underway when attacked by Japanese aircraft.

notified. If the weather report called for "east wind, rain," it meant US–Japanese negotiations had broken down and code machines in the United States were to be destroyed in preparation for war. That message also gave the Hawaii Operation task force a green light to attack.

The Japanese Navy had details on Pearl Harbor. As the harbor was in plain view of the city, and visitors could take aerial sight-seeing trips over the naval basin and near most military posts, espionage was a matter of looking, recording and keeping track of naval traffic, as opposed to sneaking onto military reservations. Within a few months, a spy at the Japanese embassy had a complete record of all vessels stationed at Pearl, their schedules, which ships were under repair, which had left for sea duty, and the disposition of aircraft. The spy passed Tokyo this information.

Alerted by Washington, Kimmel and Short passed the order for extra vigilance on November 27. Hawaii was easy duty and, if the truth were known, somewhat dull, as are most routine peacetime military stations. Men complained about the food, the weather, pay-day, duty rosters, and so on. War seemed distant from Hawaii.

Still, Gen. Short was concerned about sabotage, and he ordered all army aircraft to be bunched together so they could better be guarded: however, this also made them sitting ducks for an air assault. He ordered munitions secured, coastal artillery put on alert, and radar stations shut down at 0700 hrs. Admiral Kimmel started rotating carriers in and out of the harbor and set up ship and naval aircraft patrols. Vessels were alert for submarine threats to shipping. The aircraft carrier *Lexington* was ordered to take aircraft, which Kimmel felt were sorely needed at Pearl, to Midway. Despite precautions, no one really dreamed of an air attack. Warships, yes; sabotage and possibly an invasion force, yes; but air attack? No one gave it much credence.

US government cryptographers monitored Japanese transmissions. Washington, while still neutral, agreed with London that the Allies would concentrate on defeating Germany first. London was given three of the ultra-secret MAGIC decoders, but Pearl Harbor did not receive any. Moreover, because of the "defeat Germany first" mentality, men and materiel which could have bolstered the Pacific operations were diverted to the Atlantic. Fifty lend-lease destroyers, which the US Navy could readily have used, were sent abroad.

Despite the shadow of war, life went on as usual in Pearl Harbor. Generally speaking, ships on maneuvers returned in time to spend the weekend at their berths in the harbor. Although supposedly a third of the fleet was out at any one time, sometimes comings and goings overlapped. Pearl Harbor was the strongest base in the Pacific, and the first way-station from the mainland to the Orient. Artillery protected the coastline and, although some older aircraft were there, twelve B-17s augmented Oahu's capability. Japan viewed Pearl Harbor as the number-one threat to security.

Opening moves

Although he did not know the significance of the date, Nomura was told to complete negotiations by November 22. He requested an extension from Tojo and was told: "There are reasons beyond your ability to guess why we want to settle Japanese–American relations by the 25th." The message granted an extension until November 29, stating that this deadline "absolutely cannot be changed. After that, things are automatically going to happen." Nomura could not know that the deadline coincided with the sailing of the Southern Operation task force. War was his shadow, gaining substance as the likelihood of peace waned.

Japanese naval vessels slipped out of anchorage in twos and threes to rendezvous at Tankan Bay in Etorofu (in the Kurile Islands) on November 22, 1941. They would sail on November 26, following a

Oahu was the first leg of the journey for the China Clipper. Like many of the military amphibians or seaplanes, the Clipper was moored in shallow waters adjacent to shore. The ANZAC Clipper was about 200 miles east of Oahu when the attack started and diverted to Hilo, Hawaii.

Pearl City

EAST LOCH

MIDDLE LOCH

Beckoning Point

Mokunui
Island

Mokuiki
Island

65 aircraft in total stationed
here, including PBYs, OS2Us,
SU3s, J2Fs & SOC-1s

Aircraft Hangars
(for utility planes)

Aircraft Parking Area

Ford Island

Pearl Harbor NAS

Oil Storage
Tanks

Runway

Control
Tower

Gasoline Wharf

Seaplane
Ramps

Kuahua

Waipio Peninsula

Water
Tower

Seaplane &
Patrol Hangars

Seaplane
Ramps

Dredge

Floating
Drydock

Ten Ten Pier

Hammer-head
Crane

Crane

SOUTHEAST LOCH

US Naval
Reservation

Merry's
Point

Hospital Point

Drydock No 3
Drydock No2
Drydock No 1

Water
Towers

District HQ

Navy Yard

Naval
Hospital

Oil
Storage
Tanks

WEST LOCH

Consolidated
Barracks

Waipio Point

Hickam
Air Force Base

N

Bishop Point

Hawaiian
Air Depot
Hangars

Aircraft Parking Strip

0		500 yds
0		500 m

28

No. = ship's number
c. = date commissioned
conv. = date converted
DD = destroyer
CA = heavy cruiser
CL = light cruiser
SS = submarine
CM = minelayer
DM = light minelayer
DMS = fast minesweeper

YMS = minesweeper
PT = motor torpedo boats
AD = destroyer tender
AV = seaplane tender
AH = hospital ship
AK = cargo ship
AO = oil tanker
AR = repair ship
AX = auxiliary ship
PG = patrol gunboat

BB = battleship

northerly route to avoid accidental sightings by vessels and aircraft which operated on a more southerly route. The destroyers would be refueled daily and major vessels every fourth day. Winter seas were rough, and little sea traffic strayed that far north of the equator; still, the accompanying forward destroyer screen had orders to sink any vessels, to keep their secret at any cost. Once under way, the fleet would maintain radio silence, and dummy transmissions from near the Japanese mainland would maintain the illusion for Allied listening posts that the task force was still in Japanese waters.

The Hawaii Operation

The Japanese military plan had three phases. Phase one was to surprise Pearl Harbor, neutralize the American fleet, and to extend the perimeter to include Wake Island, the Gilberts, the northern Solomons, most of New Guinea (a threat to Australia), Java, Sumatra, Malaya, Burma (east to the Indian border), Thailand, the Philippines, and Borneo. Phase two was to strengthen military presence of the new perimeter. Phase three was defensive: to protect the perimeter and destroy any incursions from the outside.

Simultaneous army and navy attacks were to batter Pearl Harbor, the Philippines, and Malaya. The army would land on the latter two and thrust towards Java. Wake Island, Thailand, Guam, and Hong Kong would also be occupied by the army. Two destroyers, *Ushio* and *Sazanami*, would shell Midway, and carriers returning from Pearl Harbor would complete the reduction of any defenders on Wake. Although there was no overall commander, army and navy attacks would be simultaneous: one swift thrust and the ripe fruits of the Pacific would fall into Japanese hands.

Preparations

The plan called for a concentrated assault using dive-bombers, high altitude bombing, and torpedo attacks. Bombers began practice runs, both high altitude and dive-bombing. The pilots' scores constantly improved and their hit ratios soared. Torpedo bombers began practicing, but their scores were less impressive, and although Genda did everything within his power, there was a barrier his men could not break, no matter how much they practiced. The harbor was too shallow for the conventional torpedoes then in use.

The US knew of the successful British torpedo attack at Taranto but they did not put out torpedo nets in Pearl Harbor: they were extremely time-consuming to erect and it was generally accepted that the harbor was too shallow for conventional torpedoes to function. This false sense of security was heightened by Pearl's seemingly impregnable defenses, which rendered sea bombardment an unlikely eventuality.

Japan identified bombing and torpedo runs as the most effective way to destroy the ships of the US fleet, based on British success at Taranto. The major problem, however, was that Japanese Model II torpedoes penetrated too deeply into the water, and thus would stick in the mud of the shallow harbor.

Fuchida, Genda, and Murata insisted that torpedo attacks in waters up to 33 feet deep must improve. Generally the attackers dropped torpedoes which followed a depth of approximately 65 ft. With practice,

Akagi launched all her aircraft against Pearl Harbor. Here, Zero number AI-108 takes off. Each aircraft had a distinctive ID showing its carrier of origin: AI, *Akagi*; AII, *Kaga*; BI, *Soryu*; BII, *Hiryu*; EI, *Shokaku*; and EII, *Zuikaku*.

the pilots improved, but they could not achieve the 33 feet requirement. Almost despairing, they studied the situation, and eventually devised an innovative solution; the use of torpedoes with added wooden fins. These would give them additional stability and provide enough extra buoyancy to strike targets successfully in shallow waters. The torpedoes sank to only 39 ft. on average, but they operated on a straight and narrow course – a double improvement. Once they began fitting wooden fins and practicing with them, scores for kills in maneuvers rose dramatically to 70 percent, and higher on stationary vessels. (In 1944, after two years of torpedo pilot losses, scores were barely 15–18 percent.)

Yamamoto now had torpedoes that would function in shallow Pearl Harbor, and although delivery was planned for near the end of November, they had overcome their major hurdle. Following a concerted effort, the torpedoes were functioning satisfactorily by mid-November, and delivery by ship was guaranteed. The plan for a torpedo attack thus moved from theory to reality.

Initially at 10 percent, Japanese bombing scores rose steadily to 80 percent when both pilot and bombardier were made responsible for scoring a hit. (By 1944, pilot attrition had dropped bombing scores to 11 percent.)

For identification purposes, the Japanese had broken Pearl Harbor into district areas: A (between Ford Island and the Navy Yard); B (the northwest area of Ford Island); C (East Loch); D (Middle Loch); and E (West Loch). District A was subdivided into five areas: the docks northwest of the Navy Yard; the area mooring pillars; the area Navy Yard repair dock; the docks; and the remaining area. On a target constructed to resemble Pearl Harbor, they practiced their attack runs.

As of December 3, the Japanese knew *Oklahoma, Nevada, Enterprise,* two heavy cruisers, and 12 destroyers had left Pearl Harbor, and five battleships, three heavy cruisers, three light cruisers, 12 destroyers, and a seaplane tender had arrived. There seemed to be no unusual activity to suggest that the US was preparing for an attack, and shore leaves were being granted as usual. On December 4, the disposition of ships was the same, and no undue air traffic was noted. As of December 5, *Oklahoma* and *Nevada* arrived in the harbor and *Lexington* and five cruisers departed: the total ships reported in harbor were eight battleships, three light cruisers, 16 destroyers and four Honolulu class light cruisers, as well as five destroyers. *Utah* and a seaplane tender reentered the harbor. Furthermore, the report showed that no defensive balloons were up, no blackout was enforced, no anti-torpedo nets had been deployed, and there were no evident patrol flights. *Enterprise* was at sea on maneuvers. Life at Pearl Harbor followed a leisurely pace, as if there was no inkling of a Japanese attack.

Each part of the Pearl Harbor task force had responsibility for specific areas and targets: Air Attack Force (the carriers *Akagi*, *Kaga*, *Hiryu*, *Soryu*, *Shokaku*, and *Zuikaku*), 1st Air Fleet, air attacks; 1st Destroyer Squadron (17th Destroyer Division, *Nagara* flagship and 18th Destroyer Division, *Akiguma* flagship), screening and escort; 3rd Battleship Division (3rd BB Division and 8th Cruiser Division), screening and support; 2nd Submarine Division (I-17 flagship, I-21 and I-23), patrol; 7th Destroyer Division, the attack on Midway air base; 1st Supply Unit (*Kyokuto Maru* flagship, *Kenyo Maru*, *Kokuyo Maru*, and *Shikoku Maru*) and 2nd Supply Unit (*Tohu Maru* flagship, *Toei Maru*, and *Nippon Maru*), daily refueling.

A composite prewar photo showing aircraft superimposed above USS *Enterprise* in October, 1941. On December 7, *Enterprise* was 200 miles west of Oahu, heading home after delivering aircraft to Wake Island.

A6M2 Model 21 (Zero, or Zeke)

D3A1 Model 11 (Val)

D3A1 MODEL 11 (VAL)
Purpose:
Two-seater carrier and land based dive-bomber
Specification:
Engine: 1000 hp Mitsubishi Kinsei 43, or 1070 hp Mitsubishi Kinsei 44, engine
Maximum speed: 237 mp/h (430 km/h)
Climbing speed: 3,000 miles (9,845 ft) in 5 min 48 sec
Range: 915 statutory miles (1,464 km), 795 nautical miles
Armament: two 7.7 mm forward-firing machine guns, one 7.7mm flexible
rearward-firing machine gun. Provision for an external bombload of 370kg (816 lbs)
Dimensions: wingspan – 14.37m (47 ft. 1.5in). Length – 10.2m (33 ft. 5.5 in).
Height – 3.847m (12 ft. 7.5 in).
Max Take-off Weight: 8,047 lbs (3,650 kg)

Nakajima B5N2 Type 97 (Kate)

NAKAJIMA B5N2 TYPE 97 (KATE)
Purpose:
Three-seater carrier borne and land-based torpedo and level bomber
Specification:
Engine: one 1,115 hp Nakajima Sakae 21 radial engine.
Maximum speed: 229 mp/h (368 km/h)
Climbing speed: 3,000 miles (9,845 ft) in 7 min 40 sec
Range: 609 miles (980 km)
Armament: one 7.7mm trainable Type 89 machine gun in rear cockpit. External variable
bomb load, or one torpedo, to a maximum of 800 kg (1,764 lbs).
Dimensions: wingspan – 15.52m (50 ft., 11 in). Length – 10.3m (33 ft., 9.5 in).
Height – 3.7m (12 ft. 1.75 in).
Max Take-off Weight: 8,157 lbs (3,700 kg)

A6M2 MODEL 21 (ZERO, OR ZEKE)
Purpose:
Long range carrier and land based single engine fighter
Specification:
Engine: Nakajima NK1C Sakae 12 Engine
Maximum speed: 331 mp/h (532 km/h)
Climbing speed: 3,000 miles (9,845 ft) in 9 min 30 sec
Range: 1,927 statutory miles (3,101 km), 1,675 nautical miles
Armament: two 20mm cannon and two 7.7 mm machine guns, with provision for two
132lb bombs
Dimensions: wingspan – 12m (39.37 ft.). Length – 9.06m (29.72 ft.).
Height – 3.05m (10 ft.).
Max Take-off Weight: 5,313 lbs (2,410 kg)

1 – FLIGHT HELMET
Komachi is wearing a late model Type 30 flight helmet. It is made from high quality leather cowhide fully lined with rabbit fur. Japanese naval supply depots subcontracted private Japanese civilian companies such as Takashimaya-Iida or Nagata Shoten in order to manufacture these items for the war effort.

2 – FLIGHT GOGGLES
His flight goggles have maroon-colored aluminum frames that are hand-sewn onto a padded velveteen cushion. The cat-eye shaped glass lenses are two ply divided by a thin clear plastic. The center plastic protects the wearer from glass particles in the event of breakage. The aluminum frames of the goggles are embossed in both upper corners with "MAN" under a halfrising sun (*Asahi*) logo which designates manufacture in the Manchurian Naval Depot.

3 – MUFFLER
His muffler is a knitted wool scarf that has been sewn in a circular tube for added warmth. The wool mufflers were issued in beige, olive drab or navy blue. Naval pilots also wore a silk muffler that was cut from discarded silk parachutes, and were worn like an ascot. Unlike their Japanese Army pilot counterparts, Japanese Navy pilots were not issued the *toque* (a balaclava, or woollen hood with an oval cut out for the face).

4 – FLIGHT SUIT
His flight suit is a one-piece winter issue. It is made from dark brown or olive drab wool gabardine material with a combination zipper and button front. On the upper left chest area of the flight suit is a half-round button pocket suitable for a handgun. An exterior 1 x 2 inch (2.54cm x 5.08cm) olive drab cloth patch is sewn above the pocket so that the user can write a name or unit designation number there. The inside lining is black, quilted cloth, and the collar is lined with rabbit fur. The flight suit is neither fireproof nor waterproof – former pilots often commented that it absorbed a lot of water, which made swimming in it difficult.

5 – FLIGHT INSIGNIA
On Komachi's flight suit is an insignia that bears a red felt wreath with a single airplane mounted on navy blue wool circular piece of cloth. This early (1930-1939) insignia designates the rank of 3rd Class Petty Officer attached to the Aviation branch, and is worn on the left sleeve. Although this insignia was used throughout the war as available, it was phased out after 1940 and replaced with the woven yellow anchor and wreath on a cotton black patch. This was primarily done to identify rank without disclosing the user's proficiency specialty. Contrary to stereotypical views, the Japanese Navy did not use flags containing the red *hinomaru* (rising sun symbol) on their flight suits during the Pearl Harbor campaign.

6 – GAUNTLET GLOVES
The gauntlet gloves are made of a high quality deerskin suede on the finger portion of the glove, and a two-ply heavy cowhide on the gauntlet section. The latter is secured at the wrists by a snap. The gauntlet came in winter or summer issue; the winter issue merely featuring the addition of a rabbit fur or goat skin lining. Each glove had a 1 x 2 inch (2.54cm x 5.08cm) olive drab cloth patch sewn to the outside portion of the gauntlet section, where the user could write their name.

7 – FLOAT VEST
The float vest or life jacket consists of tight weave cotton cloth material sewn into 22 independent sausage-shaped chambers. There are eight large upright chambers on the back and seven small and medium chambers on the left and right front of the vest. Each chamber is filled with kapok. The float vest is secured to the user by two small ties on the chest, one large wraparound tie at the waist, and a groin strap that extends from the buttocks to the front of the user. The float vest provided extra warmth, but gave a false sense of protection against flying shrapnel.

8 – PARACHUTE AND HARNESS
Komachi is wearing the model Type 97 harness and parachute seat pack. The early (prior to 1942) dark green cotton silk straps of the harness had an attached heavy nickel plated steel center snapping device with "D" rings. All were embossed with anchor inspection stamps. After 1942, the metal components were replaced with lightweight aluminum devices. The back of the harness has a green cotton canvas pad that provides added comfort for the user. The navy parachute seat pack is the same dark green with orange piping. The seat pack parachute could be attached to the harness by simply clipping the left and right quick-release hooks on the seat pack to the two left and right "D" rings on the harness near the lower rib cage position of the user.

9 – FLIGHT BOOTS
The early Japanese Navy flight boots from 1936 to 1939 were made of

Imperial Japanese Navy Pilot
Navy pilot Petty Officer 3rd Class Sadamu Komachi serving aboard the Japanese naval carrier *Shokaku* 1941–42

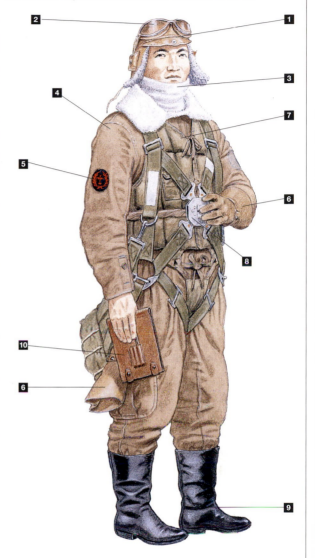

dark brown cowhide: black pairs appeared in the 1940's and were issued until late 1944. The bottom portion seam of the boot is completely rounded above the toes, where the left and right halves are joined with a center seam that extends up to the top of the boot. The Navy boots had a label sewn to the outside, where the user could write their name and the rubber soles displayed a diamond pattern.

10 – MAP CASE
Komachi is holding a penciled map case, possibly a private purchase. During a December 1998 interview, Komachi recalled using a Type 2 wooden plotting board and a Type 4 Model flight calculator that was attached above his knee with the assistance of fixed elastic strapping devices. The Type 4 calculator has a location to store a pencil and an aluminum brace to secure maps or relevant flight paperwork.

Gary Nila

"Climb Mount Niitaka"

The Pearl Harbor task force sailed on November 26 towards Pearl Harbor, radio operators listening while maintaining radio silence. Yamamoto sent Nagumo a coded message: "*Niitaka yama nobore*" ("Climb Mount Niitaka") meaning that the attacks would go forward as planned. Admiral Nagumo received a telegram on December 2, 1941 at 1700 hrs telling him to open a top-secret envelope. Inside, he found the fateful message: "Our Empire has decided to go to war against the United States, Britain and Holland in early December." The message set the date for December 8 (December 7, Pearl Harbor time). Nagumo told his officers the attack was on.

As the task force cruised onwards, the rolling winter seas it encountered seemed to symbolize the worldwide turbulence heralded by these events. For the next five days, the Japanese waited for an amendment, worried about a retraction of orders or an encounter which might tip their hand; but none came.

The day of December 7 arrived without reprieve. In Washington, Nomura was told to expect a 14-part message which had to be translated and delivered to Hull by 1300 hrs Washington time. The typist, incompetent but with the proper security clearance, was too slow, so Nomura postponed the meeting with Hull for an hour. When all was typed, Nomura headed for Hull's office. The time was 1420 hrs.

Despite Nomura's futile attempts to discover the reason for Tokyo's deadline, the designated hour passed without apparent action. US government code-breakers were still working on the message.

Just after 0800 hrs Hawaiian time, Washington received the first reports from Pearl Harbor that they were under attack, and the terrible reality struck the code-breakers, who rushed to get copies to Marshall, Hull, and others – but it was too late.

An awful sense of national helplessness, resulting in rage and determination, spread with the news reports. Suddenly, sharply, and with the jangling of an unwelcome alarm clock, Yamamoto's sleeping giant had awakened.

THE FIRST WAVE

Night darkened the sky and ocean, with only a faint demarcation between; true dawn was over an hour away. The minesweepers USS *Crossbill* and USS *Condor* patrolled 1.75 miles south of the Pearl Harbor entrance buoys. On watch aboard the *Condor* at 0342 hrs, Ens. R. C. McCloy sighted a white wake and asked Quartermaster Uttrick what he thought the object was. Through glasses, Uttrick identified it as a periscope, and at 0357 hrs contacted USS *Ward*, on entrance patrol, to investigate. Uttrick's blinker message read: "Sighted submerged submarine on westerly course, speed nine knots."

Lieutenant William Outerbridge commanded *Ward* while she patrolled the harbor entrance. A new officer on his first command, he was aware of degenerating relations between the US and Japan, and decided that what Uttrick had seen was most likely a Japanese submarine. He requested a status report from *Condor* and was told that their last sighting was at 0350 hrs and that the object was moving towards the harbor entrance. "Sound general quarters," Outerbridge ordered.

For the next hour, the USS *Ward* conducted a fruitless sonar sweep of the area. At 0435 hrs, Outerbridge had *Ward* stepped down from general quarters. The protective net to Pearl Harbor was scheduled to swing open at 0458 hrs to admit the minelayers, and would remain open until 0840 hrs. Although they did not know it, the sub probably intended to shadow the minesweeper into the safety of the harbor, a wolf sliding in among the sheep.

The sighting, although not an everyday occurrence, was not unheard of, and was logged. Ward continued her rounds. Entering the harbor after a standard tour of duty at 0458 hrs, *Crossbill* and *Condor* returned to their berths. The harbor's anti-submarine net did not close.

This photo, most probably of the *California*, gives a good view of the Number 3 turret with a catapult on top. Note also the canvasses spread over the decks, which gave crewmen protection from the sun and heat.

First light and the first wave departs; 0615 hrs, December 7. The Zero fighters were the first planes to take off from the Japanese carriers, and they circled overhead, waiting for the Kates and Vals of the first attack wave to join them. On board *Akagi*, the Japanese command carrier, Cmdr Mitsuo Fuchida (observer, accompanied by Lt. Mitsuo Matsuzaki, pilot, and Petty Officer 1/C Norinobu Mizuki) prepared to take off in Kate tail no. AI-301. Fuchida tied a *hachimaki* around his head, with the legend "Certain Victory" on it. The ship's crew had been allowed special leave from their duties to witness this historic moment. There was no more delay: the hours of destiny for the Hawaii Operation lay directly ahead. (Adam Hook)

A three-seater 'Jake' observation seaplane, tailcode JI-1, catapulted from the cruiser *Tone* at 0530 hrs. Seconds later, JII-1 from *Chikuma* also began its solo flight. They winged through the predawn towards Lahaina and Pearl Harbor anchorages respectively; their orders – survey target areas and report on the conditions, breaking radio silence. Their mission was literally the last chance for the Japanese Navy to abort the planned attack, should it be deemed necessary.

At 0530 hrs, the Japanese task force turned northeast, heading into a 28-knot wind. The carriers pitched 4–5 degrees in the decreasing 6-foot swells; but the decision had been made, and *Akagi* signaled the aircraft of the first wave to prepare for take-off at 0615 hrs.

About 250 miles north of Oahu, the first planes steadily took off from the six Japanese carriers and circled, waiting for all 183 of the aircraft in the first wave to join them. No aircraft were lost during take-off. At 0630 hrs, they took up V-formation, like homing geese, and headed south-southwest towards their primary target, Pearl Harbor naval basin. Commander Fuchida noted such pristine beauty in the early morning that he vividly recalled the scene decades later.

The sun rose on a fair Sunday, with mainly high clouds, and a sea whose swells were decreasing. West of Pearl Harbor at 0620 hrs, 18 SBDs took off from the USS *Enterprise* on a routine scouting mission to fly ahead and land at Ford Island, according to Halsey's instructions. Although aware of uneasy Japanese–US relations, this seemed a routine training mission and they planned to arrive in time for breakfast, around 0800 hrs. The *Enterprise* lay 200 miles west of Oahu and was heading home. Commander H. L. Young piloted one SBD; Lt. Cmdr Nichol, Halsey's flag secretary, flew with him.

The crew of the USS *Antares*, a supply ship, sighted what they thought was a sub and notified Ward at 0630 hrs. One of three ASW planes, a PBY, also sighted the sub and dropped a smoke marker on it just as *Ward* arrived on the scene. Lieutenant Outerbridge saw what appeared to be a submarine's conning tower breaking the surface. Though it could have been friendly, the vessel did not surface or attempt to

Many minesweepers and US Coastguard vessels (shown here) patrolled the waters off the Hawaiian chain. At the beginning of World War II, many coastal minesweepers were converted trawlers or members of the Bird class.

communicate. Following standing orders that unidentified vessels were considered hostile, Outerbridge opened fire at 0645 hrs. One round penetrated the sub's conning tower. *Ward* covered the projected course of the unknown submarine with depth charges. The PBY completed two circles, and dropped a depth charge on each pass. Without knowing it, the Americans had fired the first shots in the battle for Pearl Harbor.

The sub did not resurface, and Outerbridge thought they had hit her. At 0653 hrs, he sent coded signals to 14th Naval District headquarters, saying: "Attacked, fired upon, and dropped depth charges upon a submarine operating in a defensive area." The PBY reported to PatWing 2 headquarters as well.

Excerpt from a Japanese newsreel, showing a Kate taking off from carrier *Shokaku*. In Hawaii Operation, the carriers turned into the wind to launch the aircraft that attacked Pearl Harbor and US military installations.

Hawaiian radio stations often broadcast music all night when flights of incoming aircraft were expected from the mainland United States. This was one such night. The station's signal was loud and clear to the approaching Japanese, and at 0700 hrs Cmdr Fuchida ordered his men to use it as a directional locator. Less than five minutes later, privates Lockard and Elliott, manning the mobile US Army radar post on Opana Ridge, saw a blip on their screen, a sizable force of unidentified aircraft, 132 miles north of Oahu and closing. They wondered where the aircraft were from and if the radar station's equipment was defective. If the blip was accurate, its size indicated a group of more than 50 aircraft.

At 0710 hrs Elliott notified headquarters at Ft. Shafter but the Signal Corps telephone operator responded that all Signal Corps personnel had left for breakfast. By this time the blip was 100 miles north and closing.

The duty officers of the 14th Naval District received Outerbridge's message, which had been delayed in decoding, at 0715 hrs. About 260 miles north the second wave of the Japanese attack – 168 aircraft – took off.

At 0720 hrs, the operator called Opana Ridge radar back. Lockard answered. The operator had found an Air Corps officer, Lt. Kermit Tyler, who had observed the morning activities at the plotting boards. On listening to Lockard explain about an incoming blip, he remembered the radio had played all night and thus knew that some planes from the mainland were arriving. Lockard did not mention the size of the blip, and Tyler would not have known any difference had the size been revealed.

In Washington D.C., Kramer received the final installment of the Japanese 14-part message. It read: "The Japanese Government regrets … it is impossible to reach an agreement through further negotiations." The message was assembled and sent to Adm. Stark, and when taken to Stark, someone commented: "the virulence and tenor of the language … was enough to indicate that we could expect war." Wilkinson suggested sending an additional warning to Pearl Harbor, but the officers decided to do nothing at that time.

Bratton assembled the entire message and read it, trying to work out its significance. While he was doing so, a shorter intercept arrived from

Old Pali Pass lookout in the Koolau Range overlooks Kaneohe and was a landmark for Japanese fliers. Changed in the 1950s, the road no longer exists in this fashion.

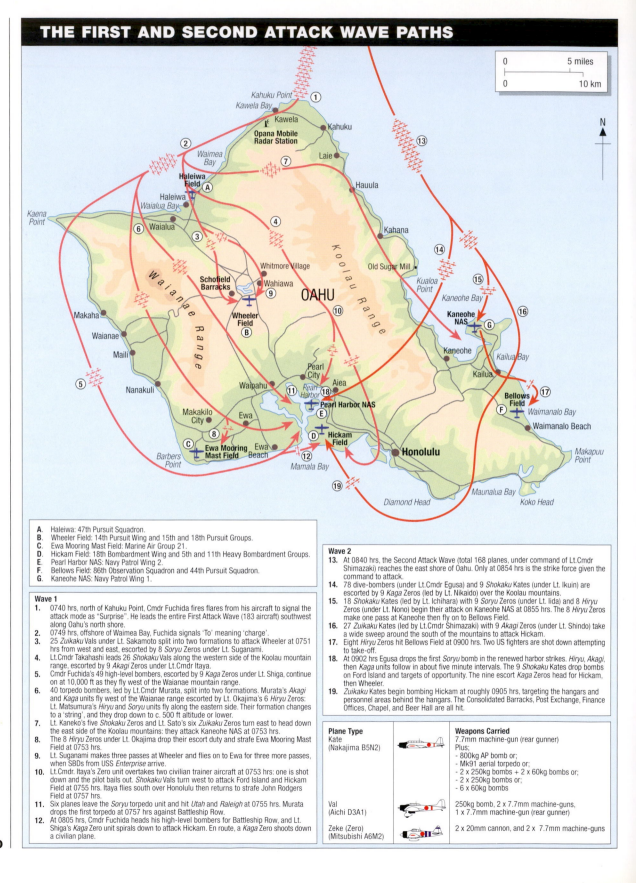

A. Haleiwa: 47th Pursuit Squadron.
B. Wheeler Field: 14th Pursuit Wing and 15th and 18th Pursuit Groups.
C. Ewa Mooring Mast Field: Marine Air Group 21.
D. Hickam Field: 18th Bombardment Wing and 5th and 11th Heavy Bombardment Groups.
E. Pearl Harbor NAS: Navy Patrol Wing 2.
F. Bellows Field: 86th Observation Squadron and 44th Pursuit Squadron.
G. Kaneohe NAS: Navy Patrol Wing 1.

Wave 1

1. 0740 hrs, north of Kahuku Point, Cmdr Fuchida fires flares from his aircraft to signal the attack mode as "Surprise". He leads the entire First Attack Wave (183 aircraft) southwest along Oahu's north shore.
2. 0749 hrs, offshore of Waimea Bay, Fuchida signals 'To' meaning 'charge'.
3. 25 *Zuikaku* Vals under Lt. Sakamoto split into two formations to attack Wheeler at 0751 hrs from west and east, escorted by 8 *Soryu* Zeros under Lt. Suganami.
4. Lt.Cmdr Takahashi leads 26 *Shokaku* Vals along the western side of the Koolau mountain range, escorted by 9 *Akagi* Zeros under Lt.Cmdr Itaya.
5. Cmdr Fuchida's 49 high-level bombers, escorted by 9 *Kaga* Zeros under Lt. Shiga, continue on at 10,000 ft as they fly west of the Waianae mountain range.
6. 40 torpedo bombers, led by Lt.Cmdr Murata, split into two formations. Murata's *Akagi* and *Kaga* units fly west of the Waianae range escorted by 6 *Hiryu* Zeros: Lt. Matsumura's *Hiryu* and *Soryu* units fly along the eastern side. Their formation changes to a 'string', and they drop down to c. 500 ft altitude or lower.
7. Lt. Kaneko's five *Shokaku* Zeros and Lt. Sato's six *Zuikaku* Zeros turn east to head down the east side of the Koolau mountains: they attack Kaneohe NAS at 0753 hrs.
8. The 8 *Hiryu* Zeros under Lt. Okajima drop their escort duty and strafe Ewa Mooring Mast Field at 0753 hrs.
9. Lt. Suganami makes three passes at Wheeler and flies on to Ewa for three more passes, when SBDs from USS *Enterprise* arrive.
10. Lt.Cmdr. Itaya's Zero unit overtakes two civilian trainer aircraft at 0753 hrs: one is shot down and the pilot bails out. *Shokaku* Vals turn west to attack Ford Island and Hickam Field at 0755 hrs. Itaya flies south over Honolulu then returns to strafe John Rodgers Field at 0757 hrs.
11. Six planes leave the *Soryu* torpedo unit and hit *Utah* and *Raleigh* at 0755 hrs. Murata drops the first torpedo at 0757 hrs against Battleship Row.
12. At 0805 hrs, Cmdr Fuchida heads his high-level bombers for Battleship Row, and Lt. Shiga's *Kaga* Zero unit spirals down to attack Hickam. En route, a *Kaga* Zero shoots down a civilian plane.

Wave 2

13. At 0840 hrs, the Second Attack Wave (total 168 planes, under command of Lt.Cmdr Shimazaki) reaches the east shore of Oahu. Only at 0854 hrs is the strike force given the command to attack.
14. 78 dive-bombers (under Lt.Cmdr Egusa) and 9 *Shokaku* Kates (under Lt. Ikuin) are escorted by 9 *Kaga* Zeros (led by Lt. Nikaido) over the Koolau mountains.
15. 18 *Shokaku* Kates (led by Lt. Ichihara) with 9 *Soryu* Zeros (under Lt. Iida) and 8 *Hiryu* Zeros (under Lt. Nono) begin their attack on Kaneohe NAS at 0855 hrs. The 8 *Hiryu* Zeros make one pass at Kaneohe then fly on to Bellows Field.
16. 27 *Zuikaku* Kates (led by Lt.Cmdr Shimazaki) with 9 *Akagi* Zeros (under Lt. Shindo) take a wide sweep around the south of the mountains to attack Hickam.
17. Eight *Hiryu* Zeros hit Bellows Field at 0900 hrs. Two US fighters are shot down attempting to take-off.
18. At 0902 hrs Egusa drops the first *Soryu* bomb in the renewed harbor strikes. *Hiryu*, *Akagi*, then *Kaga* units follow in about five minute intervals. The 9 escort *Kaga* Zeros head for Hickam, then Wheeler.
19. *Zuikaku* Kates begin bombing Hickam at roughly 0905 hrs, targeting the hangars and personnel areas behind the hangars. The Consolidated Barracks, Post Exchange, Finance Offices, Chapel, and Beer Hall are all hit.

Plane Type	Weapons Carried
Kate (Nakajima B5N2)	7.7mm machine-gun (rear gunner) Plus; - 800kg AP bomb or; - Mk91 aerial torpedo or; - 2 x 250kg bombs + 2 x 60kg bombs or; - 2 x 250kg bombs or; - 6 x 60kg bombs
Val (Aichi D3A1)	250kg bomb, 2 x 7.7mm machine-guns, 1 x 7.7mm machine-gun (rear gunner)
Zeke (Zero) (Mitsubishi A6M2)	2 x 20mm cannon, and 2 x 7.7mm machine-guns

Tojo to Ambassador Nomura. This stated: "Will the Ambassador please submit to the United States Government … our reply at 1:00pm. on the 7th, your time." Bratton tried to reach Marshall but was unable to do so until 1030 hrs Washington time. Kramer almost casually noted that with the time differential involved, it would be 0730 hrs Pearl Harbor time.

General Marshall's telegram to Short arrived at RCA in Honolulu but was not identified as a priority message and was given to RCA Messenger Tadao Fuchikami at 0733 hrs. He was to deliver it to Short's HQ in the normal course of his morning rounds.

At 0738 hrs, a reconnaissance "Jake" from *Chikuma* gave a visual confirmation that the main US fleet was in Pearl Harbor: "Enemy … at anchor, nine battleships, one heavy cruiser, six light cruisers." The pilot related conditions important to the approaching first wave: "Wind direction from 80°, speed 14m, clearance over enemy fleet 1,700m, cloud density seven." The recon aircraft from Tone reported: "Enemy … not in Lahaina anchorage." Although brief, the message had tremendous overtones, because all hopes and plans for catching the Americans at the deep-water Lahaina anchorage (off Maui Island, 80 miles southeast of Oahu) were dashed, and confirmed that the attack would concentrate on the shallow Pearl Harbor anchorage. Their new torpedo modifications would get their baptism of fire. Having reported, the pilot swept wide to the south, trying to find the carriers; but he did not fly west, and *Enterprise* remained undiscovered.

By 0739 hrs at Opana Ridge, Elliott and Lockard had lost the incoming blip because of the ground clutter pattern caused by the hills behind Opana Ridge. A minute later, Fuchida dropped below the clouds and sighted the northern shore beneath Oahu's empty skies: no enemy aircraft. Fuchida felt relieved that the attack was going according to plan: a quick surprise thrust.

At 0749 hrs, Fuchida ordered his pilots to deploy into attack formation by firing a single shot from his flare gun, signifying "torpedo planes to attack." His radioman tapped out the signal "To-To-To" (the first syllable of *tosugekiseyo*, meaning "to charge"). Then Fuchida thought Lt. Cmdr Itaya may have missed his signal and fired a second shot. Lieutenant Commander Takahashi saw both shots and misunderstood, thinking dive-bombers were to strike: he ordered his dive-bombers into immediate attacks. Lieutenant Commander Murata observed both shots and then saw Takahashi's plane (EI-238) gliding into attack formation. He knew there had been a misunderstanding, but it could not be rectified, so he led his torpedo group into its attack pattern.

Torpedo forces split into two strings. Eight planes under Lt. Matsumura, flying BII-320, and followed by eight under Lt. Nagai, closed on their targets on the northwest side of Ford Island. Twelve torpedo bombers under Murata, piloting AI-311, and followed by 12 under Lt. Kitajima, flying AII-311, angled south then east over Hickam Field and then up to Battleship Row. Aircraft reduced altitude and flight leaders singled out the designated target. If a target was questionable, pilots and bombardiers were ordered to make passes until they had reasonable certainty of a hit. If they could not acquire their target, they could then elect to strike another.

Wheeler Field, eight miles from Pearl Harbor, was a primary target in the Japanese attack plan. Once the ships were in flames, Americans

A 1940 US Army field communications unit. A radar unit, housed in two trailers, was on Opana Ridge, where the approaching Japanese aircraft were first noticed; but they were later dismissed as incoming B-17s.

would think of retaliation. If airfields were destroyed, there would be little or no retaliation. Flood had ordered nearly 100 U-shaped bunkers built to house aircraft and protect them from air attack. General Short, however, had ordered that planes be massed to protect them from sabotage. There were no trenches and no anti-aircraft, as that was not Flood's responsibility but the Department's. Wheeler Field was a sitting duck. When Japanese aircraft reached it, American aircraft were neatly grouped on runways and aprons. Suganami's *Soryu* Zeros banked and came in low, guns blazing. Planes, quarters, PX, the administration building and the golf course were shredded by gunfire. As Flood said, the attackers were so close "I could even see the gold in their teeth."

At 0751 hrs, bombs began to fall from *Zuikaku* Vals on Wheeler Field. P-40 Bs and Cs were lined up with the obsolete P-36s outside the hangars. With the element of complete surprise, the Japanese aircraft swept in systematically to attack ground targets: aircraft, hangars, base buildings. The attacks followed the same dreadful pattern: first bombers released payloads and then circling Zeros strafed the field and buildings. Men of the 14th Pursuit Wing sought to push undamaged aircraft to safety while Japanese aircraft dived on them repeatedly. Many tires were shot flat, and hangars storing munitions were set ablaze. When one plane was hit, the volatile aviation fuel ignited, sending up a fountain of flame. Like as not, the adjacent aircraft was damaged and its fuel was also leaking. A second later it, too, would ignite, damaging the next aircraft, and so on down the line until the runway was lined with blazing aircraft.

Diamond Head, seen from the north, with Honolulu in the foreground. Many Japanese pilots used the distinctive landmark during their approach for the attack on Pearl Harbor.

Kaneohe and Ewa Mooring Mast Field came under attack at 0753 hrs, and Fuchida radioed the task force on a broad band: "*Tora, Tora, Tora*" ("Attack-Destroy"), indicating that so far their approach had been a complete success and the US naval and army installations had been caught unaware.

Suganami's *Soryu* fighters made three strafing runs at Wheeler between dive-bomber runs, then headed towards Ewa Field to relieve Okajima's *Hiryu* Zeros attacking the marines. They made repeated passes at the American aircraft on the ground. As at Wheeler, bullets ruptured fuel tanks, which ignited. Fuel spilled from bullet holes, and rivulets of aviation gasoline streamed from damaged aircraft to others which were crackling and threatening to explode. The fire truck tried to reach the aircraft to salvage ammunition and guns, but Japanese strafers blew out its tires and it ground to a halt.

Fuel spilled in streams, setting fire to tents and even to the sand which soaked it up. The second wave of attack came just over half an hour later, savaging tents, burning hulks, the hospital, other buildings, and personnel. One brave marine fired his .45 cal. pistol at Japanese aircraft in frustration. On the ground, a group of marines manhandled a scout plane, used it as a machine-gun platform, and opened fire on their attackers. The Japanese strike force roared away, leaving Wildcats blazing, scout bombers burning, and utility aircraft destroyed. Their losses? One Zero.

When the Japanese attacked Kaneohe, the OD notified Bellows Field, who thought he was making them the butt of a practical joke – until 0830, when the Japanese hit Bellows too. When Cmdr Harold M. Martin reached Kaneohe it was too late. The 33 PBYs on the base were sitting ducks (three more were in the air). The anti-aircraft batteries that should have been there had been returned to army bases on the previous Friday afternoon. Four PBYs were moored less than 1,000 yards apart, and four more were inside Hangar 1. Zeros struck first, gliding

0757 HRS: *Akagi* and *Kaga* Torpedo Attack Units approach Battleship Row from the southeast: Lt. Cmdr Shigeharu Murata and Lt. Kazuyoshi Kitajima lead them. A total of 24 Kates, armed with Mk 91 torpedoes, descend to attack. The intended targets are key US ships, among the most important in the Pacific Fleet. The *Nevada*, *West Virginia*, *Oklahoma* and *California* are all torpedo targets.

0753 HRS: 26 *Shokaku* Val dive-bombers, under Lt. Cmdr Kakuichi Takahashi, approach from the east. The targets are the aircraft stationed at Hickam Field and Pearl Harbor NAS on Ford Island.

CinCPAC HQ

SOUTH-EAST LOCH

AIEA BAY

7

8

FORD ISLAND

6

5

EAST LOCH

3

4

KEY TO US SHIPS
(Refer to the map of the harbor on pages 28–29 for full details of US ship positions.)
1 Ramsay, Gamble, Montgomery
2 Trever, Breese, Zane, Perry, Wasmuth, Medusa, Curtiss
3 Tangier, Utah, Raleigh, Detroit
4 Aylwin, Dale, Farragut, Monaghan
5 Ralph Talbot, Patterson, Henley
6 Phelps, MacDonough, Worden, Dewey, Hull, Dobbin, Solace, Allen, Chew
7 Phoenix, Blue, Whitney, Conyngham, Reid, Tucker, Case, Selfridge
8 Battleship Row: Nevada, Vestal, Arizona, Tennessee, West Virginia, Maryland, Oklahoma, Neosho
9 Bobolink, Vireo, Rail, Tern
10 Helena, Oglala

PEARL CITY

THE FIRST ATTACK WAVE, PEARL HARBOR, 0750–0810 HRS

All was quiet in Pearl Harbor on Sunday, December 7. Routine duties were being performed, and the sun was starting to climb in the sky. But the following two hours would bring chaos and carnage to the normally tranquil harbor. At 0755 hrs, the 1st Attack Group, consisting of 89 Kates under Lt. Cmdr Mitsuo Fuchida, struck the harbor: torpedoes raced to their targets, then bombs began to fall. The US Pacific Fleet was caught unawares in these early hours, with a violent and rude awakening.

0755:30 HRS: Two *Shokaku* squadrons of eight and nine Val dive-bombers respectively (led by Lt. Masao Yamaguchi and Lt. Hisayoshi Fujita) hit Hickam Field, and begin their deadly, steep descents. Their targets are the hangar line and the aircraft parked outside on the apron.

0805 HRS: *Akagi*, *Kaga*, *Soryu* and *Hiryu* Attack Units (led by Lt. Cmdr Mitsuo Fuchida) reach the harbor, having approached from over Barber's Point (farther south) to disguise their attack path and avoid detection over land. They total 49 Kates, armed with 1,800lb bombs. The units release their deadly load over the ships on Battleship Row, maintaining their altitude as horizontal bombers high above the harbor. Fuchida's attack plan is to hit the single ships *California* and *Nevada* and inboard ships *Maryland*, *Tennessee*, and *Arizona* of Battleship Row. *Pennsylvania* in dry dock is ignored by Fuchida's high-level bombers which carry the unique bomb designed for such a target:

Bomber attack formation:
Akagi 15 Kates (Cmdr Fuchida)
Kaga 14 Kates (Lt. Cmdr Takahashi Hashiguchi)
Soryu 10 Kates (Lt. Heijiro Abe)
Hiryu 10 Kates (Lt. Cmdr Tadashi Kusumi)

HICKAM FIELD

NAVY YARD

WAIPIO POINT

9

TENTEN PIER

HOSPITAL POINT

WEST LOCH

PEARL HARBOR NAS

BECKONING POINT

2

WAIPIO PENINSULA

1

MIDDLE LOCH

N

0756 HRS: Also targeted by *Soryu* and *Hiryu* Torpedo Attack Units are ships berthed at TenTen Pier in the Navy Yard. The Japanese hope to find and sink a key US ship at this long pier (called 'TenTen' because of the 1010 ft length of the nearby dry dock): however, the light cruiser *Helena* is moored here. The minelayer *Oglala* is berthed beside her – but she does not provide protection from the torpedo strike, as Nagai's torpedo passes under *Oglala*.

0755 HRS: Nine Vals from Lt. Cmdr Kakuichi Takahashi's *Shokaku* unit swoop down on Ford Island Naval Air Station, targeting the hangars and the exposed aircraft on the sea ramps and apron.

0755 HRS: *Soryu* and *Hiryu* Torpedo Attack Units, with 16 Kates armed with Mk 91 torpedoes, under command of *Hiryu* Lt. Hirata Matsumura, spearhead the surprise strike on the harbor. Having split off from the *Akagi* and *Kaga* torpedo units, they are to target the key ships on the northwest side of Ford Island. The intended targets are the carriers normally berthed on this side of Ford Island: however, the only ships here are *Utah*, *Tangier*, *Raleigh*, and *Detroit*, and some of the berths are vacant too. *Soryu* leader Lt. Tsuyoshi Nagai and Lt. Matsumura view target ship *Utah* for what it is, but six *Soryu* Kates depart from Nagai's formation to attack her. One misses and hits *Raleigh*; two of the others hit Ford Island itself.

Ford Island, and the battleships *West Virginia* and *Oklahoma*, were first hit by the Japanese around 0758 hrs. Ramsey saw the explosions and ran to com-center to transmit a local warning: "Air raid, Pearl Harbor. This is NO drill!"

down low and strafing, bullets chewing up tarmac and ripping through planes. The field's fire truck was also destroyed. Martin had not yet reached his headquarters when the first PBY was ablaze in the water.

Japanese first-wave attack aircraft descended on Ford Island and Hickam airfields. Torpedo bombers began their runs on Battleship Row. Pearl Harbor was under attack. On this particular Sunday morning all was SOP – business as usual – in the Pacific Fleet. Chapel services were planned, mess halls and galleys were laying out breakfast, launches to and from shore were readying, and men on duty rosters were preparing for their watch. Japanese aircraft swooped out of the morning sky, lining their sights on capital ships. At 0755 hrs, Lt. Cmdr Logan Ramsey stood at the window of Ford Island Command Center watching the color

Captured after the war, this photo shows two Kates (center and top right) as a torpedo hit geysers upward from *Oklahoma* (center, far side of Ford Island). *Raleigh* and *Utah* (far left, on the near side of Ford Island) spout smoke. (David Aiken)

Smoke from the Navy Yard (left) and Ford Island (center) rises while anti-aircraft bursts dot the skies during the attack. Although surprised, naval vessels reacted as quickly as possible, so that when the second wave arrived, it was severely challenged.

guard hoist the flag. A plane buzzed by and he snapped, "Get that fellow's number!" Then he recalled, "I saw something … fall out of that plane …" An explosion from the hangar area cut his words short. Racing across the hallway, Ramsey ordered the radioman to send out the following message: "Air raid, Pearl Harbor. This is NO drill." The message went out on the local frequencies at 0758 hrs.

In a moment the scene of battleships and tenders preparing for morning services, mess call and watch changes was transformed to battle alert. Torpedo planes nosed down, leveling and dropping their deadly loads into the water. Wakes streaked towards berthed vessels. Observers were confused, surprised, and horrified as the nature of the situation dawned. Rear Admiral W. R. Furlong aboard the *Oglala*, which was berthed in the *Pennsylvania*'s normal position, saw a bomb fall from one of the approaching aircraft. He made a mental note that the flyer would be in trouble with his CO, when the plane banked and Furlong saw its insignia – a Rising Sun! "Japanese!" He yelled: "Man your stations!"

Ensign R. S. Brooks aboard *West Virginia* saw what he erroneously thought was a shipboard explosion on *California*. Reacting instantly, he ordered hands to turn to for an Away Fire and Rescue Party. Men boiled up from bunks to help.

Lieutenant Matsumura recognized USS *Utah*, the former battleship now a training ship, on the northwest side of Ford, so he searched for alternate targets. Six planes from Lt. Nagai's formation saw *Utah* and sped like arrows to drop their torpedoes at 0755 hrs. *Utah* and *Raleigh* reeled under torpedo explosions. Aboard *Raleigh*, confusion reigned. The torpedo knocked out electrical power just as a bugler sounded battle stations. Sailors immediately manned *Raleigh*'s 3-inch guns, which had ammo in ready boxes, while she began listing to port.

South of Ford Island, TenTen Pier experienced a slashing attack. Nagai headed into the sun towards a battleship but realized after launch it was the paired *Oglala* and *Helena*. Nagai's torpedo went under *Oglala* and the *Helena* shook as the torpedo bit into her starboard side. *Oglala*'s seams split from the concussion and took on water.

On Ford Island NAS, Kingfishers, Catalinas and other naval aircraft were savaged. In the background, smoke rises from the damaged battleship *Nevada*, while a bright plume of smoke billows skyward as *Shaw* explodes.

At 0757 hrs, on Battleship Row, Lt. (JG) Goto flew to the left rear of Murata and straight at *Oklahoma*, released his torpedo and climbed. "It hit!" cried his observer as a huge jet of water geysered upward.

Aboard the *Vestal* outboard of *Arizona*, CWO Hall saw the bombers, identified them as Japanese and sounded general quarters. Men poured from below decks and the mess area, and within ten minutes *Vestal*'s guns were firing at the invaders.

About 0800 hrs, crewmen Huffman and de Jong of PT 23, a Higgins class 78-ton patrol torpedo boat, saw aircraft (identified as Japanese by the "meatball" Rising Sun insignia on their wings) swooping in and dropping bombs and torpedoes. They argued about what the aircraft were doing, awakening Ensign Ed Farley, who had been sleeping below deck after a late night on the town. Farley made his way to the deck, wiping sleep from his eyes and yawning. Following their gaze, he was horrified to see one plane fly over them on dead course for *California*: an instant later the battleship was rocked by an explosion. Huffman and de Jong jumped into a gun turret and fired on the attacking aircraft with twin .50 cal. machine guns. One attacking aircraft wobbled and then went down, possibly the first blood the American anti-aircraft fire had drawn.

Across the navy basin, on the shore opposite the sub base, *Ramapo* was in the process of loading six additional PT boats in cradles for transport to the Philippines. When the attack began, crews of the PT boats tried to man their guns, but the turrets would not move because the engines had been shut down for transport. No engines, no power, no movable turrets. Crewmen began rotating turrets by muscle power, while gunners turned barrels red-hot with fire. Boats in cradles already on *Ramapo*'s deck were especially vulnerable – neither on land nor in

The *Arizona* was the worst hit. Slammed by two bombs, she quickly sank, taking over 1,200 seamen down with her. Half the US casualties at Pearl Harbor were on this one vessel.

An SBD-2 Dauntless dive-bomber from USS *Enterprise* in prewar colors. The legend in front of the fuselage cocarde identified the plane. These dive-bombers flew into the shooting match between vessels and attackers on the morning of Sunday, December 7.

the water – as attackers blasted vessels and dived with guns chattering.

Southwest of *Oklahoma*, *California* rocked in the water as two port-side torpedoes struck home. Acting decisively, Ens. Edgar Fain ordered counter-measures to prevent capsizing. The USS *Nevada*'s band played while the flag was being raised at 0800 hrs. They heard the dull and constant thudding of distant bombs; one or two nearby vessels seemed to have gone crazy, firing their guns. The *California* quivered when another torpedo impacted.

About 0805 hrs, Cpt. Shoemaker, commander of Ford Island, gritted his teeth and stared at the seaplane apron and hangar which was blazing "like a forest fire." Only a few seaplanes were undamaged, and Shoemaker organized work crews to move undamaged ones away from those that were burning.

The USS *Oklahoma*, outboard of the *Maryland*, was staggered by torpedo hits. Men rushed to ammo lockers, only to find them secured. Once lockers had been forced open, there was no compressed air to power the guns, and the ship had begun to list markedly when more torpedoes knifed home. Rescue parties began pulling sailors from below, up shell hoists and to the deck, while her executive officer, Cmdr J. L. Kenworthy, realized she was in danger of capsizing. At the eighth torpedo hit, he gave the order to abandon ship by the starboard side and to climb over the side onto the bottom as it rolled over. In the harbor, nearly 150 crewmen were on *Oklahoma*'s side when the ninth torpedo hit her. As one crewman said, *Oklahoma* "bounced up and … settled down … turned over": the battleship slowly rolled until her barnacled bottom saw daylight.

Lieutenant Commander F. J. Thomas was the ranking officer aboard *Nevada* and Ensign J. K. Taussig, Jr. was officer of the deck and acting air defense officer when general quarters sounded. Taussig ran to the nearest gun. At 0805 hrs, *Nevada* blasted a torpedo plane that was approaching on its port beam beginning a torpedo run. *Nevada*'s five-inch guns and .50 cal. machine guns poured fire into the aircraft. The burning torpedo plane managed to release its torpedo. The silvery streak sliced the water and threw up a white wake on an intersect course with *Nevada*. The explosion punched a hole in *Nevada*'s port bow: compartments flooded and she began to list to port. Japanese bombers dropped their payloads near her port quarter at 0830. Thomas ordered counter-flooding. Burning fuel oil from *Arizona* drifted towards *Nevada*, and Thomas ordered her underway to avoid it. Meanwhile, Taussig was hit in the thigh and refused aid while he commanded a gun crew. Lieutenant Ruff came aboard from a launch. He suggested Thomas manage *Nevada*'s action from below decks and Ruff would manage them from above. Smoking and listing, *Nevada* struggled towards the harbor entrance.

Suddenly, *Vestal*, a repair ship moored outboard of *Arizona*, opened fire. *Vestal* had fires blazing around her and seemed likely to catch fire. At 0805 hrs, a bomb hit *Arizona* aft of No. 4 turret and one hit *Vestal* forward, and both convulsed.

Until now, outboard vessels had suffered the majority of the torpedo damage, but high above the harbor the drone of bombers closed. Then

bombs began falling on inboard ships at Battleship Row from high above.

As *Oklahoma* capsized, *Arizona* and *Vestal* were struck again at 0806, and the *Arizona*'s explosion knocked men off nearby vessels due to the might of the concussion: the bomb pierced her forward magazine, and the explosion was so powerful that damage control parties aboard nearby *Vestal* were blown overboard when a fireball erupted skyward from *Arizona*'s magazine. Immediately, *Arizona* began settling. Fires aboard *Vestal* were extinguished like someone blowing out a match when *Arizona*'s magazine exploded. The *Arizona*'s bridge was aflame and she was settling like a rock. Her explosion showered the harbor with debris, body parts and survivors. Many men were hopelessly trapped below deck in an instant. Over 1,200 died with her in that devastating moment, including Adm. Kidd and Cpt. Van Valkenburg. Lieutenant Commander Fuqua realized that *Arizona* was "no longer in fighting condition" and ordered survivors to abandon ship. *Arizona* had received two bombs; as of 1032 hrs, the ship was a hulk.

When fire-fighting crews tried to man the hoses at Ford Island, there was no water pressure. *Arizona* lay on the water mains. An alert ensign turned on the fire sprinkler system and wetted down fuel storage tanks on the tank farm. Across from the tanks, *Neosho*'s anti-aircraft batteries peppered the sky in front of incoming aircraft. After *Oklahoma*'s roll, *Neosho* made preparations to get underway. She had emptied her high octane aircraft fuel load just minutes before the first air strike, yet many thought she would immolate nearby vessels, including *Maryland*, *Tennessee*, and *West Virginia*. Slowly, *Neosho*'s stacks fumed, and she moved away from anchorage at 0842. By 0900 hrs, *Neosho* had cleared Battleship Row and the oil tanks on Ford Island. She had four near misses and reached Merry's Point in Southeast Loch at 0930 hrs.

Sirens blared. All across the harbor, shipboard intercoms and PAs blasted out general quarters. Aircraft were ordered up to seek out the enemy. Sluggishly, vessels began to respond, smoke pouring at first slowly and then steadily from their stacks and their sporadic anti-aircraft fire dotted the skies, which were filled with aircraft displaying the Rising Sun. The target ship *Utah* began to settle, turning over: a shuddering *Oklahoma* had capsized. Damage control parties aboard *Raleigh* fought to keep her afloat and upright while the first wisps of oily smoke from a score of vessels rose into the morning sky.

At 0800 hrs, twelve stripped-down, unarmed B-17s flying singly from the mainland United States (which Tyler thought were the unidentified radar blip) sighted Oahu and began their descent. Meanwhile, the eighteen recon SBDs from the USS *Enterprise* commenced their approach to Ford Island. Some were stitched by enemy aircraft, and hungry American anti-aircraft batteries also sought them out. Enemy and friendly aircraft mixed, while undiscriminating anti-aircraft fire reached to slap them all from the skies.

Admiral Kimmel observed the beginning of the attack from his home. He summoned his driver and rushed to headquarters. Commander Daubin of Sub Squadron Four went with him. Kimmel arrived at CinCPAC HQ and watched helplessly as plane after plane dived, wheeled, and circled like vultures above the now-smoking ships in the anchorage. He later said: "My main thought was the fate of my ships."

In the midst of the fighting, one SBD from *Enterprise* landed. Young and Nichol deplaned on the pitted runway as anti-aircraft fire dotted the sky. "They're shooting at my own boys," Young yelled, pointing at his incoming recon group: "Tell Kimmel." American fire knocked one SBD into the sea, but its crew was rescued. Zeros shot down four. One SBD was hit by a Val, and its crew is still missing. Another landed at Kauai on Burns Field. The remainder reached Ford or Ewa later in the day: they would be refitted and sent hunting for the Japanese fleet.

Captain Landon's B-17s from the mainland were due to land at Hickam at any moment. Base commander Col. Farthing was in the control tower, waiting with Cpt. Blake, his operations officer, who was to guide in the aircraft. A swarm of planes topped the horizon from the north, flying low and fast. Some bypassed Hickam and flew towards Ford Island, but seven bombers made a beeline for Hickam Field.

Lieutenant-Colonel James Mollison was at home when the attack began. He rushed outside and saw the planes make their initial passes; then he ran inside, dressed and went to headquarters. Once there, he called Short's office in Oahu to report that they were under attack. To emphasize his point, he held the receiver so Phillips (Short's chief of staff) could hear the bombs exploding.

Bombs splintered the Hawaiian Air Depot, a B-24 on the transit line, and two more hangars. The Zeros seemed to single out the mighty B-17s, and 7.7 mm bullets rent the Flying Fortresses where they were parked. Captain B. E. Allen could not get all four engines of his B-17 to crank, but he taxied his aircraft away from the others which were being savaged. Ground crewmen were able to taxi several planes away from the flames.

Landon's B-17s reached Hickam as the attack was getting into full swing. Manned by skeleton crews, unarmed and low on fuel after their long flight from the mainland, they flew blindly into a turkey shoot. Some

0755:30 HRS: Lt. Masao Yamaguchi led his eight *Shokaku* Val dive-bombers to bomb the hangar line from the east. In one blast, 22 men on the apron, routinely preparing a B-18 for a training flight, are killed. Hangars 7 and 11 are hit.

0910 HRS: 27 Kates from *Zuikaku* (6th Attack Unit, led by Lt. Cmdr Shigekazu Shimazaki) reach Hickam and begin to shower the hangars and barracks with 550lb bombs. The Consolidated Barracks receives direct hits.

0755:30 HRS: Nine *Shokaku* Val dive-bombers (led by Lt. Masao Yamaguchi) sweep in from the north, and rain destruction on the hangars and aircraft on the apron. A B-24A being prepared for a secret mission over Japanese Mandates is destroyed in the first bomb hit. Hawaiian Air Depot and hangars 13 and 15 take direct hits, and are badly damaged.

HAWAIIAN
AIR DEPOT

CONSOLID
BARRAC

BASEBALL
FIELD

PARAD
GROUN

A   B   C   D

US B-1

TAXI

0810 HRS: Anti-aircraft fire from USS *Helm* and Fort Kamehameha, to the south of Hickam, brings down Takashi Hirano's Zero fighter (he is Lt. Cmdr Itaya's wingman) as he pulls up over the channel entrance leaving Hickam. It crashes at Fort Kamehameha. Their work done, the Japanese fighters move on to hit Ewa Mooring Mast Field further west.

0800-0900 HRS: Four B-17Cs and eight B-17Es (38th Recon Squadron and 88th Recon Squadron, flying from California) attempt to land at Hickam. Under attack from confused US friendly fire and Japanese fighters, eight manage to touch down with damage. Two head for Haleiwa on the north of Oahu. One tries landing at Bellows Field but runs over a ditch, wiping out its landing gear. Another is chased around Oahu, eventually landing on a civilian light aircraft runway next to a golf course.

0807 HRS: Outside Hangar 5, Cpt. Raymond Swenson's B-17 lies burning, broken in two along the fuselage. Lt. Cmdr Itaya has shot up Swenson's plane, and this ignites flares in the bomber's radio compartment. It skids down the runway on fire, before coming to rest outside the hangar where it breaks in two.

THE ATTACKS ON HICKAM FIELD ARMY AIR BASE, 0755–0920 HRS

Home to the 18th Bombardment Wing (a huge potential threat to the Japanese fleet), Hickam Field was quiet this Sunday morning. Ground crews were preparing for the arrival at 0800 hrs of a flight of 12 B-17s from California. However, the arriving aircraft that flew into Hickam just before 0800 hrs were intent on a different kind of wake-up call. In total, Hickam's losses in terms of men were considerably higher than in Oahu's other air bases, and the Japanese destroyed over one-third of the base's total aircraft. By 0930 hrs, 45 ambulances were on the scene: many of the injured were treated at Tripler General Hospital.

OIL TANK FARM

0800 HRS: Nine Zeros from Lt. Cmdr Itaya's *Akagi* Fighter Unit, fresh from strafing John Rogers Field, make three strafing circles each, targeting the hangars and apron.

0805 HRS: Once the high-level bombers are committed to their runs, Lt. Yoshio Shiga leads nine *Kaga* Zeros to join the melee. Ground crews report people being chased down the streets behind the barracks by firing planes. During strafing, a *Kaga* fighter hits its belly tank on Hickam's runway but gets airborne enough to crash in the ocean south of Oahu.

0910 HRS: Nine Zeros under Lt. Saburo Shindo, from the carrier *Akagi*, subject the base to three strafing attacks. Ground crews frantically try to ready their planes, to get a counter-attack under way – but the Zeros target them too.

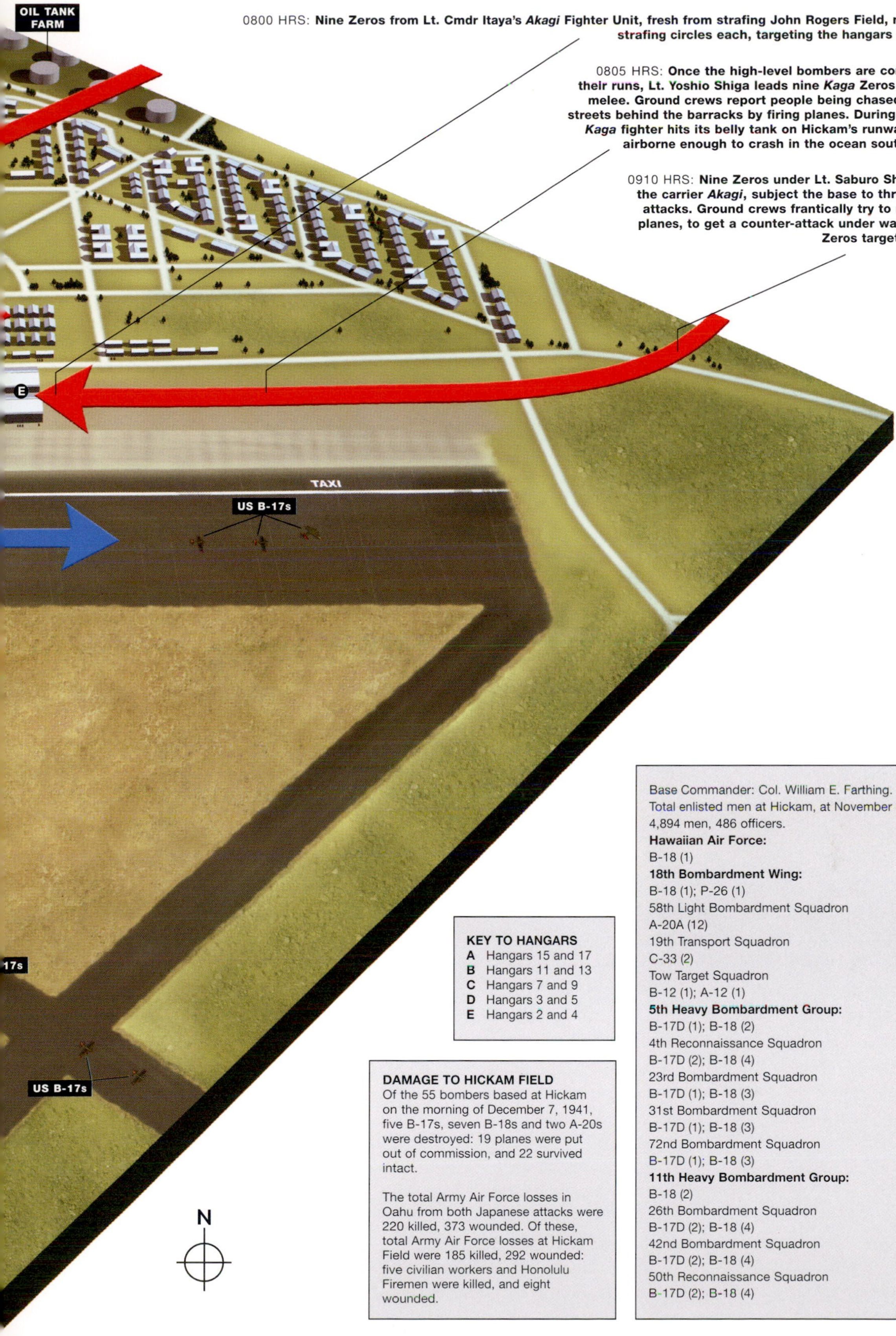

E

TAXI

US B-17s

17s

US B-17s

N

KEY TO HANGARS

A Hangars 15 and 17
B Hangars 11 and 13
C Hangars 7 and 9
D Hangars 3 and 5
E Hangars 2 and 4

DAMAGE TO HICKAM FIELD

Of the 55 bombers based at Hickam on the morning of December 7, 1941, five B-17s, seven B-18s and two A-20s were destroyed: 19 planes were put out of commission, and 22 survived intact.

The total Army Air Force losses in Oahu from both Japanese attacks were 220 killed, 373 wounded. Of these, total Army Air Force losses at Hickam Field were 185 killed, 292 wounded: five civilian workers and Honolulu Firemen were killed, and eight wounded.

Base Commander: Col. William E. Farthing.
Total enlisted men at Hickam, at November 30, 1941: 4,894 men, 486 officers.
Hawaiian Air Force:
B-18 (1)
18th Bombardment Wing:
B-18 (1); P-26 (1)
58th Light Bombardment Squadron
A-20A (12)
19th Transport Squadron
C-33 (2)
Tow Target Squadron
B-12 (1); A-12 (1)
5th Heavy Bombardment Group:
B-17D (1); B-18 (2)
4th Reconnaissance Squadron
B-17D (2); B-18 (4)
23rd Bombardment Squadron
B-17D (1); B-18 (3)
31st Bombardment Squadron
B-17D (1); B-18 (3)
72nd Bombardment Squadron
B-17D (1); B-18 (3)
11th Heavy Bombardment Group:
B-18 (2)
26th Bombardment Squadron
B-17D (2); B-18 (4)
42nd Bombardment Squadron
B-17D (2); B-18 (4)
50th Reconnaissance Squadron
B-17D (2); B-18 (4)

Japanese aircraft ignored the grounded planes and, guns blazing, made straight for the incoming B-17s. The latter headed off in all directions to escape their attackers. Three Japanese Zeros latched on to Landon's tail as he landed, shot and shell bursting around him. Other B-17 pilots were under attack, from friend and foe alike, as they tried to land all over the island. All made it to one airfield or another. When the smoke cleared, more than half the aircraft at Hickam were burning or shattered hulks.

At 0755 hrs, Cpt. Frank W. Ebey of the 55th Coast Artillery at Fort Kamehameha dropped the book he was reading when the first attack started and yelled for his sergeant to get the machine guns working. The guns were set up on the tennis court and blazing away at the attackers by 0810 hrs. They and USS *Helm*, heading out to sea, both hit Zero leader Itaya's wingman who faltered and went down at Fort Kamehameha.

The US Army Air Corps had all manner of aircraft at its various airfields, including this obsolete open cockpit P-26 Peashooter at Wheeler Field. Its lineage from the racing aircraft of the early 1930s is evident.

Station KGMB interrupted its broadcast and transmitted: "All army, navy and marine personnel, report to duty!" Back in the harbor, *West Virginia* began to list strongly to port when she was struck twice, the bombs coming so close together that one felt almost like the aftershock of the other, setting her No. 3 turret aflame. Captain Bennion at *West Virginia*'s bridge was nearly eviscerated by shrapnel from a hit on nearby *Tennessee* and collapsed, mortally wounded. Lieutenant White and Mess Attendant Doris Miller (fleet boxing champion) were ordered to move Bennion to safety. On arrival, they had no stretcher for transport. Miller and Lt. White were ordered to man two machine guns while waiting for a stretcher. A pharmacist's mate tended Bennion's wound and made him comfortable and answered questions about the battle until Bennion died moments later. Before the end of the day, *West Virginia* was to take nine torpedoes and two bomb hits.

At 0812 hrs, Kimmel sent a message to the Pacific Fleet and Washington, DC: "Hostilities with Japan commenced with air raid on Pearl Harbor." Three minutes later, KGMB transmitted another message, repeating the call for all military personnel to report to duty stations.

In the harbor, all had been caught unawares, like sitting ducks. However, through the smoke and flame came a sight to give hope to all the sailors and personnel witnessing the devastation: a destroyer had fought its way clear of the smoke and was heading towards the mouth of the harbor. The USS *Helm* was making her run to the open sea and, exited Pearl Harbor at 0817 hrs, spotted a small sub outside the entrance. *Helm* fired on the sub but missed. The sub hit a reef, struggled, and freed itself, submerging while *Helm* fired fruitlessly.

The time was 0825 hrs. In Honolulu the fire department had been deluged with calls for assistance and had responded to Hickam Field. Enemy aircraft strafed the fire-fighting vehicles, killing four fire-fighters and wounding six. Five minutes later, KGMB sent out a third call for military personnel to report to base.

In Honolulu, rumors abounded. Civilians, military personnel, government leaders, Hawaiian, Caucasian and Japanese-American, young and old, stood wide-eyed at the scene in the harbor. Some

Staff Sergeant Lee Embree, aboard a B-17, photographed the crash of a Japanese dive-bomber just before two more made a strafing pass on his plane.

thought the explosions and low-flying aircraft were an Army Air Corps training exercise; others thought oil tanks on the base must have exploded. Still others realized that the island was under attack and feared imminent invasion. Many citizens watched the "air show" over Pearl Harbor and Schofield, not realizing the situation. Stray rounds and a few bombs hit the city, jarring civilians out of their stupor. Police warned citizens to stay calm and return to their homes. After getting under way from East Loch, the destroyer *Monaghan* headed southwest towards the harbor entrance. Local radio stations sent out the first reports saying that Pearl Harbor was under attack by enemy aircraft with Rising Sun markings.

Admiral Kimmel was watching the battle when a spent bullet shattered his office window, hitting him in the chest and knocking him backwards a few steps. Men standing nearby were astounded to see Kimmel slowly bend over and pick up the spent round. He studied it for a while and then pronounced: "It would have been merciful had it killed me."

THE SECOND WAVE

There was no real break between the first and the second waves of attack, just a momentary pause in the battering before the rain of death resumed. Oily smoke streamed skywards from many of the ships; vessels listed or displayed rust-streaked bottoms when they capsized; and the incoming second wave could have used the smudge on the sky as a beacon, had it been unsure of the target area.

In Pearl Harbor's East Loch, Lt. Cmdr Bill Burford of the destroyer *Monaghan* was moving her south-southwest, heading for the sea to find and support *Ward*. Smoke from damaged ships clouded the waterway, and other vessels determined to reach the safety of open sea were in various stages of getting under way and clogged the narrow seaward corridor. Ahead, *Curtiss* was moored in Middle Loch and signaled *Monaghan* that a Japanese submarine had been sighted. *Curtiss'* 5-inch and .50 cal. guns fired on the sub at 0839 hrs. One shell tore through the conning tower, no doubt killing the commander. Noting *Curtiss'* actions, the *Monaghan* tried to fire as well but could not bring her guns

The battleships *West Virginia* and *Tennessee* were moored next to each other. Japanese aircraft repeatedly struck both of them, wreathing the battleships and the vessels which aided them in billowing clouds of oily smoke.

to bear: a moment later one of the watch reported seeing two torpedo wakes broaching the surface. Other nearby craft fired at the sub, and *Monaghan* set herself on a collision course with it. The sub was wounded and surfaced just in time for *Monaghan* to slam along the side of it. After hitting the sub, *Monaghan* dropped a depth charge on the spot despite the chance that Burford might damage his own stern. In attempting to ram the sub, *Monaghan*'s course took her directly toward Beckoning Point, where she grazed a dredge at its berth, sustaining light damage. She backed out, as other destroyers passed her, and made the open sea just as the second wave arrived.

If the first wave was smooth and took little damage, the second wave bore the brunt of the US resistance. Although initially surprised and mauled, the remaining US air defenses were determined to even the score.

Two American pilots, Lieutenants George Welch and Kenneth Taylor, had danced and then played poker the remainder of the evening before at Wheeler. Tired, they heard the first crackle of gunfire and thumps of nearby bombs at 0751 hrs. Running outside, they saw low-flying aircraft with red Rising Suns on their wings. Calling Haleiwa Field in the north of Oahu, they ordered their P-40s readied, then hopped into Taylor's car and sped towards the field. Japanese aircraft buzzed them as they drove, bullets chewing up the roadway. They raced down the winding road, not only to reach their aircraft, but to avoid strafing attacks. Perhaps if they could get aloft … Taylor and Welch hopped into their readied aircraft and took off just after 0900 hrs. Harry Brown and his roommate, John Dains, picked up the squadron XO, Bob Rogers, and were not far behind Taylor and Welch. Dains got the next P-40 in the air. A dive-bomber passed John Webster's car headed north and strafed a P-36 at Haleiwa Field. Brown and Rogers got airborne in P-36s and Webster got the next P-40.

Bellows Field suffered some damage during the attack. This P-40 attempted a pre-dawn takeoff on December 8 and collided with another plane. In the background, a soldier wearing fatigues confers with airmen.

In the harbor, USS *Alwyn* started seaward. Bombs splashed around her and she slowly surged forward, ordered to sortie. A bomb fell just short of her fantail, slamming her stern into an anchor buoy and damaging one of her screws. Aboard, only ensigns commanded *Alwyn*, all other officers being ashore. She made the open sea at 0932 hrs. Her commander pursued and tried to catch up, following her out of harbor in a launch, but she did not stop for him for fear of Japanese submarines.

At the same time, the battered battleship *Nevada* moved sluggishly away from her berth northeast of Ford Island. Smoke partly obscured visibility as her screws clawed their way towards the sea. The wind blew through her shattered bow, which sported a large gouge. Still, Thomas and Ruff were going to take her to sea, past the shattered and burning vessels on Battleship Row if they could.

Colonel Weddington at Bellows was ready for the attack. One B-17 came in with three wounded aboard. It touched down midway up the landing strip, and then ran out of runway. A lone strafer had sailed across the field at 0830 and departed. Since then, men had rushed feverishly about dispersing the 86th Observation Squadron's O-47s and O-49s, and rearming the 44th Pursuit Squadron's P-40s.

Lieutenant Commander Shimazaki's second wave arrived near Kaneohe at 0855 hrs, with 54 high-level bombers and 78 dive-bombers and 36 fighters. Fuchida was still flying over the smoking vessels and assessing damage. Fuchida stayed to view Shimazaki's results as his assessment was needed by Nagumo, who would use it to decide about another strike.

Ichihara's 18 *Shokaku* high-level bombers struck Kaneohe at 0855, escorted by Iida's nine *Soryu* Zeros and Nono's *Hiryu* Zeros. The high-level bombers made strikes down the tarmac and on the hangars. Aircraft in the hangars exploded and burned in place. After one pass, Nono took

Japanese midget (two-man) subs were ferried to Pearl aboard larger Japanese subs. This one was dimpled by a depth charge, rammed by *Monaghan*, and brought ashore for investigation.

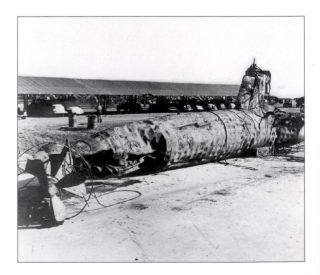

Kaneohe was attacked by Japanese aircraft that strafed not only the airstrip and hangars, but also PBYs moored dockside. Here, a PBY patrol plane burns outside a hangar.

his eight Zeros farther south to Bellows Field. At 0900 hrs, Lt. Nono's eight aircraft hit Bellows Field with six planes strafing and two serving as top cover to catch planes struggling to get aloft. O-47s were shredded by machine-gun fire, a fuel truck was ablaze, and Whiteman's 44th Squadron P-40 was downed while lifting off. Bishop got airborne as Whiteman crashed; he was easy prey for the Japanese fighters, which came in on his tail before he could gain altitude. Bishop survived when his P-40 splashed down near the beach and he waded ashore from its wreckage. The six Zeros strafed the battered B-17 past the end of the runway, but the bomber was already out of action and they were wasting ammunition on what was now a hulk.

This China Clipper was moored in much the same manner as Kaneohe's PBYs, less than 25 yards offshore. Unlike the PBYs, which were shot to pieces in the water or on runways, no Clipper was in Hawaii, though one was scheduled to arrive.

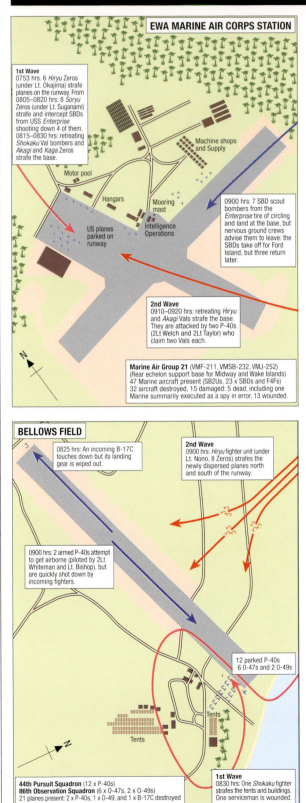

EWA MARINE AIR CORPS STATION

1st Wave
0753 hrs: 6 *Hiryu* Zeros (under Lt. Okajima) strafe planes on the runway. From 0805–0820 hrs: 8 *Soryu* Zeros (under Lt. Suganami) strafe and intercept SBDs from USS *Enterprise* shooting down 4 of them. 0815–0830 hrs: retreating *Shokaku* Val bombers and *Akagi* and *Kaga* Zeros strafe the base.

Machine shops and Supply

Motor pool

Hangars

Mooring mast

US planes parked on runway

Intelligence Operations

0900 hrs: 7 SBD scout bombers from the *Enterprise* tire of circling and land at the base, but nervous ground crews advise them to leave: the SBDs take off for Ford Island, but three return later.

2nd Wave
0910–0920 hrs: retreating *Hiryu* and *Akagi* Vals strafe the base. They are attacked by two P-40s (2Lt Welch and 2Lt Taylor) who claim two Vals each.

Marine Air Group 21 (VMF-211, VMSB-232, VMJ-252)
(Rear echelon support base for Midway and Wake Islands)
47 Marine aircraft present (SB2Us, 23 x SBDs and F4Fs)
32 aircraft destroyed, 15 damaged: 5 dead, including one Marine summarily executed as a spy in error, 13 wounded.

WHEELER FIELD

1st Wave
0751 hrs: 25 *Zuikaku* Vals under Lt. Sakamoto sweep in from the east and west and bomb the hangars and parked planes.

Barracks & Housing

Sports track

Barracks & Housing

75th Service Sqn barracks

Barracks

Hangars

Hangars

About 120 fighters parked on apron

1st Wave
0755 hrs: 8 *Soryu* Zeros, led by Lt. Suganami, serve as top cover over Wheeler, then make three strafing passes on planes on the apron.

0905 hrs: The first four 46th Pursuit Squadron P-36s get airborne, under 1Lt. Sanders, and are vectored to Kaneohe NAS. Moments later another 46th PS pilot, 2Lt. Malcolm Moore, gets another P-36 airborne and flies to the north shore area to join up with 47th PS pilot 2Lt. Harry Brown from Haleiwa Field. 0920 hrs: 2Lt. Welch and 2Lt. Taylor land at Wheeler to refuel and rearm their P-40s.

2nd Wave
0915 hrs: Seven of Lt. Nikaido's *Kaga* Zeros make a short strafing pass on Wheeler as they head home. 0930 hrs: 16 retreating *Kaga* dive-bombers, under Lt.Cmdr Makino, begin to strafe Wheeler. Welch and Taylor take off in opposite directions and join the Val formations, claiming two kills. Taylor chases another Val north of Oahu, while Welch flies solo to Ewa Mooring Mast Field area for another battle.

Main US Army Air Force fighter base on Oahu
14th Pursuit Wing: B-18, A-12, P-26, O-47, OA-8
15th Pursuit Group: P-40B/C, P-26, OA-9, AT-6
18th Pursuit Group: B-12, A-12, P-40B/C, P-36, P-25, OA9, AT-6
145 aircraft present; 42 are destroyed; 56 out of commission.

BELLOWS FIELD

0825 hrs: An incoming B-17C touches down but its landing gear is wiped out.

2nd Wave
0900 hrs: *Hiryu* fighter unit (under Lt. Nono, 8 Zeros) strafes the newly dispersed planes north and south of the runway.

0900 hrs: 2 armed P-40s attempt to get airborne (piloted by 2Lt Whiteman and Lt. Bishop), but are quickly shot down by incoming fighters.

12 parked P-40s
6 0-47s and 2 0-49s

Tents

Tents

44th Pursuit Squadron (12 x P-40s)
86th Observation Squadron (6 x O-47s, 2 x O-49s)
21 planes present: 2 x P-40s, 1 x O-49, and 1 x B-17C destroyed

1st Wave
0830 hrs: One *Shokaku* fighter strafes the tents and buildings. One serviceman is wounded.

The attacks on the airbases on Oahu were of vital importance. Had significant numbers of US aircraft been able to get airborne and respond in a co-ordinated manner, their retaliation might have left the Japanese task force, isolated at sea, open to a devastating counter-attack.

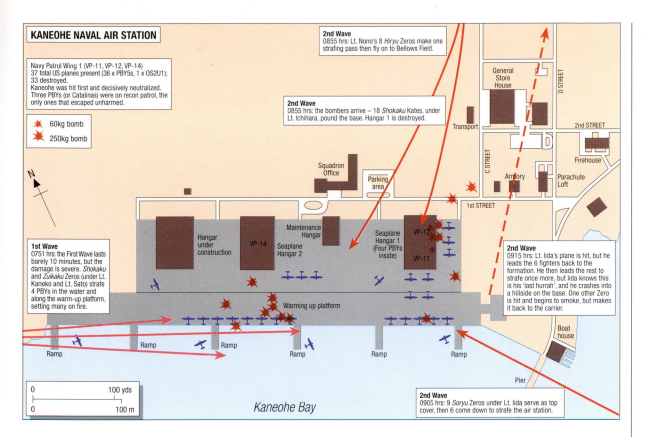

KANEOHE NAVAL AIR STATION

Navy Patrol Wing 1 (VP-11, VP-12, VP-14)
37 total US planes present (36 x PBY5s, 1 x OS2U1);
33 destroyed.
Kaneohe was hit first and decisively neutralized.
Three PBYs (or Catalinas) were on recon patrol, the
only ones that escaped unharmed.

✹ 60kg bomb

✹ 250kg bomb

N

2nd Wave
0855 hrs: Lt. Nono's 8 *Hiryu* Zeros make one
strafing pass then fly on to Bellows Field.

2nd Wave
0855 hrs: the bombers arrive – 18 *Shokaku* Kates, under
Lt. Ichihara, pound the base. Hangar 1 is destroyed.

General
Store
House

D STREET

Transport

2nd STREET

C STREET

Squadron
Office

Parking
area

Armory

Firehouse

Parachute
Loft

1st STREET

1st Wave
0751 hrs: the First Wave lasts
barely 10 minutes, but the
damage is severe. *Shokaku*
and *Zuikaku* Zeros (under Lt.
Kaneko and Lt. Sato) strafe
4 PBYs in the water and
along the warm-up platform,
setting many on fire.

Hangar
under
construction

VP-14

Maintenance
Hangar

Seaplane
Hangar 2

Seaplane
Hangar 1
(Four PBYs
inside)

VP-12

VP-11

2nd Wave
0915 hrs: Lt. Iida's plane is hit, but he
leads the 6 fighters back to the
formation. He then leads the rest to
strafe once more, but Iida knows this
is his 'last hurrah', and he crashes into
a hillside on the base. One other Zero
is hit and begins to smoke, but makes
it back to the carrier.

Warming up platform

Boat
house

Ramp

Ramp

Ramp

Ramp

Ramp

Pier

0   100 yds
0   100 m

Kaneohe Bay

2nd Wave
0905 hrs: 9 *Soryu* Zeros under Lt. Iida serve as top
cover, then 6 come down to strafe the air station.

The attack on Kaneohe NAS was
particularly devastating, and the
base suffered a high level of
damage. A combination of
strafing attacks by Zeros and
high-level bombing from Kates
ensured that almost all the PBYs
stationed there were destroyed.
(By kind permission of Mr. John
S. Kennedy, author of *The
Forgotten Warriors of Kaneohe*)

Gordon Jones and his brother Earl had been stationed at Kaneohe on December 2, 1941, and yet only five days later they were to have their baptism of fire. Between the first and second waves, they were kept busy trying to extinguish fires and moving less-damaged planes to safer locations. When the attack began, they had no reason to suspect that the second wave would be any different to the first, as Gordon recalls: "When this new wave of fighters attacked, we were ordered to run and take shelter. Most of us ran to our nearest steel hangar … this bomb attack made us aware that the hangar was not a safe place to be … several of us ran north to an abandoned Officer's Club and hid under it until it too was machine gunned. I managed to crawl out and took off my white uniform, because I was told that men in whites were targets. I then climbed under a large thorny bush … for some reason I felt much safer at this point than I had during the entire attack." For most of the men at Kaneohe, there was little else they could do but take cover until the devastating assault had passed.

Chief Ordnanceman John William Finn, a navy veteran of 15 years service, was in charge of looking after the squadron's machine guns at Kaneohe, but Sunday, December 7, was his rest day. The sound of machine-gun fire awoke him rudely though, and he rapidly drove from his quarters to the hangars and his ordnance shop to see what was happening. Maddened by the scene of chaos and devastation that he saw, he set up and manned both a .30 cal. and a .50 cal. machine gun in a completely exposed section of the parking ramp, despite the attention of heavy enemy strafing fire. He later recalled: "I was so mad I wasn't scared." Finn was hit several times by bomb shrapnel as he valiantly returned the Japanese fire, but he continued to man the guns, as other sailors supplied him with ammunition. John Finn was later awarded the Congressional Medal of Honor for his valor and courage beyond the call of duty in this action. Even after receiving some first aid treatment, he insisted on returning to his post to supervise the rearming of the returning PBYs that had escaped the devastation at Kaneohe.

Firemen trying to fight the blazes also came under strafing attack. One fire truck was hit and crashed into a hangar, exploding and setting fire to the hangar. The mission was not to be a complete success for Lt. Iida though: his plane suddenly waffled, having been hit by US fire, and streamed fuel. One look at his instruments and Iida knew he was in trouble. He banked, signaling to a fellow pilot and pointing down to the ground, indicating that he was going to crash into the enemy. Iida's Zero skimmed over the armory building (probably the intended aim of his dive) to crash into the hill behind, near the officer's quarters. Flipping, it skidded upside down before jamming into the embankment. Some believed Iida was probably dead before his plane hit the ground. Arthur W. Price, stationed at Kaneohe that morning, recalls the plane crashing: "We managed to recover some paperwork from his plane. Included was a map … We later learned that it indicated our water tank was a fuel farm. Those pilots had just peppered the hell out of that tank during the attack but couldn't set it on fire. I think that sort of confused them."

Eighteen US servicemen and a civilian were killed in the attack on Kaneohe that day: they were buried the following day on Mokapu Point on the east side of the NAS. A ceremony was also held for Lt. Fusata Iida on December 8 at Kaneohe. His body was sent back to Japan after the war.

Despite the loss of Iida's plane, the attack on Kaneohe achieved its aims. Three PBYs were out on patrol, but of those remaining, 33 were destroyed. Iida's fellow fighters began to re-form, to fly to Wheeler when holes opened in their aircraft – they were under attack! US fighters with blazing machine guns were coming after them. Four pilots from 46th Pursuit Squadron, including 1st Lt. Lewis Sanders, had also managed to get airborne in their P-36s from Wheeler and were vectored to Kaneohe. Iyozo Fujita, Iida's second in command, shot down Gordon Sterling's P-36, but left the battle heavily damaged with two other damaged Zeros. On the north shore two more P-36s attacked and he could not come to the aid of his men who were shot down. Fujita was barely able to make it back to *Soryu*. Sterling and his P-36 are still missing off Kaneohe.

Nikaido's nine *Kaga* Zeros flew on to Ford Island with nine *Shokaku* bombers, peeled off to strafe Hickam to support Shindo, then on to Wheeler Field.

Shindo's nine *Akagi* fighters escorted Shimazaki's *Zuikaku* bombers around the south coast of Oahu thence to Hickam. The bombers arrived, laying a carpet of explosives on Hickam. When anti-aircraft was occupied with the high altitude aircraft, Shindo brought his fighters down to just above rooftop level, making a pass on the installation and strafing dispersed aircraft, technical buildings and offices.

The *Zuikaku* bombers were rocked by anti-aircraft fire. They sought to hit the Consolidated Barracks with its mess hall. Above the clouds, they flew through the barrage of anti-aircraft to drop their deadly cargo. Some fell short to hit a baseball diamond, a few fell beyond to hit the parade ground. At their altitude, proper visual target identification was exacting under the best conditions, and now they were flying over a smudgepot while shells burst around them and tracers licked at their wing tips. More than one high-level bomber returned to its carrier with wind whistling through multiple bullet holes, but they all made it back.

Lieutenant Commander Egusa's dive-bombers, carrying their 550lb bombs, had the worst of it. Their job was dirty: finish off any unfinished business and get any battleships the first wave had missed. They had no element of surprise with them: the Americans were ready, armed and angry. As soon as they reached Oahu, flak began reaching up with greedy fingers, closing its grasp and threatening to unnerve many Japanese dive-bomber pilots. Lieutenant Abe commented: "AA barrages began … to close in. This gave me the shivers." Visibility was abysmal. The careful plans were abandoned, and instead Egusa's flyers decided to pick any target they had the opportunity to fire upon. Through the smoke and flames they dived, coming down low to try and pick out targets. They were not fearful while attacking, but more than one admitted to feeling shaky once they had dropped their bomb and headed towards their rendezvous.

Pearl Harbor was filled with burning oil, its smudgy plumes darkening the skies above the twisted metal hulks of American warships. Stragglers and survivors were taken to aid centers or headquarters. In momentary lulls between bomb blasts, when there was no anti-aircraft and just the soft whoosh and crackle of flames, it was as if a sudden deafness had affected everyone.

Egusa initiated the dive-bombing at 0905 hrs with his hit on *New Orleans*. His two wingmen dropped bombs on *Cassin* and *Downes* in dry dock. Soon the ships were aflame and had to be abandoned. Just minutes later, *Cassin* was wrenched with a magazine explosion that rolled her port side against *Downes*. Four bombs hit *Shaw* and started a

Wheeler Field and nearby Schofield Barracks were raked repeatedly by Japanese aircraft but remained surprisingly usable. The smoke comes from burning aircraft on the landing strip.

Chief Ordnanceman John William Finn was in charge of the squadron's machine guns at Kaneohe NAS. Despite great danger to himself, he set up both a .30 cal. and a .50 cal. machine gun in an exposed section of the parking ramp, as others (including 2nd Cl. PO Robert Peterson, shown here in this scene drawn from contemporary accounts) supplied him with ammunition. Finn moved between the two, but stayed longer on the .50 cal. due to the ease of reloading and the weight of its firepower. Despite being wounded several times by bomb shrapnel, he inflicted a heavy toll on the attackers, as bullets ripped through wings and fuselages. Lieutenant Iida's Zero was one of those hit, and crashed on a hillside near naval housing. (Jim Laurier)

huge fire. Another dive-bomber put a hit on *Pennsylvania*'s starboard side at 0907 hrs, doing a relatively small amount of structural damage but killing 18 and wounding 30 officers and men.

USS *Blue* started for the mouth of the harbor. Two Japanese Vals buzzed her and were met with .50 cal. fire. One went down off the channel entrance as *Blue* broke through to the open sea and began patrolling. There was a sound on sonar, and Blue responded with depth charges. A pattern of bubbles and an oily patina colored the waters for 200 feet, suggesting a hit.

The cruiser *Honolulu* came under attack at 0920 hrs. Egusa's dive-bombers pounded the berth (B17) with several bombs; one near miss caused considerable flooding aboard. Concussion from the underwater blast was so strong that *St. Louis*, which was berthed east of her (at B21), bounced in the shock wave.

Dive-bombers singled out larger ships. *Raleigh* survived the first wave, but now was wracked by a hit and a near miss aft. One bomb passed through the deck and missed *Raleigh*'s aviation fuel tanks by less than four yards. *Raleigh* reeled and threatened to capsize. Only by hard work did her commander keep her upright and afloat.

Welch and Taylor made their presence known at Ewa Mooring Mast Field. Taylor got two when he dropped into groups of strafing *Hiryu* and *Akagi* dive-bombers, first firing at the one ahead, and taking fire from one behind him. Welch also claimed two. They landed at Wheeler to refuel and rearm.

Vestal and *Oglala* were in trouble. Fire threatened *Vestal* and she had to move or risk immolation. A tug nosed the repair ship away from the burning *Arizona*. *Vestal* moved heavily through the water and began to list to starboard. At 0905 hrs, Young said *Vestal* was "in bad shape – we had better beach her." She nosed onto a coral reef at Aiea at 0945 hrs. *Oglala* was not so fortunate. Moored outboard of *Helena* at TenTen Pier,

This was the scary sight seen by those at Pearl Harbor as a Japanese Val with open dive brakes banked and came towards them. Black anti-aircraft dots the sky, but the Val flies through it unharmed. Note the proximity to the camera: many Vals came in very low and fast, a factor depending on the bravery and skill of the pilot.

Seen from Ford Island, a damaged *Nevada* is down at the bow but her funnel is smoking as she moves away from Ford and down the channel, attempting to reach the relative safety of the open sea.

While *Nevada* (her turrets visible to the bottom right) battled shipboard fires, a tug came alongside to give aid (foreground to the right). A direct hit on the magazine of the destroyer *Shaw* sent flames and debris skyrocketing.

her seams split by the concussion of the torpedo that hit *Helena*, and she was slowly listing. At 0930 hrs, her decks were too angled to walk on and Furlong ordered the crew to abandon ship. She capsized soon afterwards, settling on her port side. Just afterward, the USS *Shaw* bucked like a bronco when multiple explosions from the fire on board blew off her entire bow. A tower of debris went skyward and fell as far away as Ford Island, where her bugle was found.

Through the oily smoke poked a battered bow: *Nevada* was making her run south. Minutes earlier she had picked up a few floating survivors

When the Japanese attacked, Battleship Row became a shooting gallery. *Oklahoma* (left) has capsized, *Maryland* is behind her, and the burning *West Virginia* (right) has sunk next to the damaged *Tennessee*.

Just after 0900 hrs, the *Nevada* passed TenTen Pier in her run for safety towards the open sea. She had already sustained one torpedo hit at berth, but now the second wave of Japanese planes (Val dive-bombers, led by Lt. Saburo Makino from the carrier *Kaga*) swooped in to attack her. Some came from the southwest, some attacked her from the southeast, the aim being to split the American AA fire. The attack was concentrated and she was hit several times. Thomas, her acting commander, decided to beach her on Hospital Point shortly afterwards, to avoid the risk of blocking the channel and preventing other ships from escaping. (Adam Hook)

from *Arizona* as she was gaining momentum. Only a few vessels moved in the harbor, but she was one of them. She may have been down, but she was not out. Makino's *Kaga* Vals saw Nevada abreast TenTen dock and realized what she was attempting. This was too good to be true: a target, a battleship at that, and one which could bottle up the harbor if they could sink her. Coming lower, 23 Vals homed on *Nevada*. She took a dozen bomb hits as the *Kaga* unit singled her out for destruction. Eight bombs fell near her, their explosions sending splinters into her side and geysers of water sluicing over her decks. It appeared that she would escape without further damage when one last bomb exploded in front of her forecastle, slaying many sailors and jarring the whole vessel with a shudder that slammed teeth shut and knocked some men off their feet.

Thomas knew the peril. *Nevada* was responding with difficulty, and he realized she was taking on water. If she went down here, she would partially block the harbor and make undamaged vessels still in the harbor sitting targets, little more than fish in a barrel. He gave orders to turn to port and sluggishly she reacted, her bow plowing into shore at

Near the dry dock at TenTen Pier, *Cassin* and *Downes* (center rear) are smoldering. *Helena* sits beside the pier, and the dry-docked *Pennsylvania* is visible in the background. In the center, the minelayer *Oglala* has capsized.

Hospital Point, knocking sailors sprawling, and grounding *Nevada*. Her bow looked as if it had been gnawed off, and her superstructure was partly buckled – but she had not sunk! It was a minor victory, but every vessel denied the enemy was one more vessel which could later take the fight to them.

Chaos ruled the basin. Burning oil floated towards *California*; *Maryland* struggled to free herself from inboard of *Oklahoma*, which had capsized; *Arizona* smoldered; Nevada had broken free, but at a terrible price.

At about 0932 hrs, Lt.Cmdr Pullen, CO of the destroyer *Reid*, rushed through the savaged base towards the harbor, his heart heavy as he saw the ships burning and foundering. How badly mauled was *Reid*? He took his launch out to the ship and was surprised to have the officer of the deck tell him that everything was under control; then the chief engineer said that *Reid* would be able to get underway in about 30 minutes.

St. Louis' commander, Cpt. Rood, had her make way, and she began to back out. At 0940 hrs, with her engines full astern, she neared the channel. A cable securing the dredge at the south end of Ford Island blocked *St. Louis'* way. Rood ordered full speed ahead and plowed through the cable, which parted. Down the channel she sped, disregarding the normal eight-knot speed limit in harbor and certain that at any moment Japanese aircraft could sight her and attack. *St. Louis'* speed crept up to 22 knots and she cleared the harbor at 1004 hrs. Rood allowed himself the luxury of a deep breath when they reached the sea.

No doubt Rood thought *St. Louis* was clear, but then the watch saw two torpedo wakes closing with her stern. He ordered her on an immediate evasion course, and an explosion rattled her when the torpedoes hit a coral reef. A midget sub surfaced and *St. Louis'* gun crews opened fire, but the sub's conning tower had disappeared. *St. Louis* was the last ship to leave Pearl Harbor during the attack.

After bombing the harbor, Egusa's men flew towards Hickam, Wheeler, and Ewa to strafe the airfields and buildings. At Wheeler, Welch and Taylor had their fuel tanks filled and almost had the cowlings buttoned up when the *Kaga* Vals began strafing. Both got in the air and shot down two enemy just outside the base. They chased the others to claim two more. Welch flew on to Ewa and got another victory.

Shimazaki's Kates hit Hickam and were joined by dive-bombers that helped strafe hangars and aircraft on the runway. The B-17s absorbed a great deal of damage, but showed once more why they were called "Flying Fortresses." Having little more to do and needing to reach the rendezvous, Shimazaki's men headed away from the airfield. After the three passes at Hickam, Shindo broke off in his Zero and flew recon, studying the damage and assessing the effectiveness of the Japanese attack. Flying at 900 feet, he eyed the devastation. When he returned to *Akagi*, his report to Genda would be succinct: "Inflicted much damage."

At 1100 hrs, Cmdr Fuchida began his recon and assessment flight over Oahu. Carefully, he noted which ship positions were burning, which had capsized or were now low in the water, and which appeared unharmed. Fuchida stayed over the harbor, observing and rounding up stragglers. When the last aircraft of the latest wave turned west, Fuchida looked at the sun overhead and headed towards *Akagi*.

Schofield Barracks, next to Wheeler, was strafed several times in the morning. At 0950 hrs, Lt. Stephen Saltzman, communications officer of

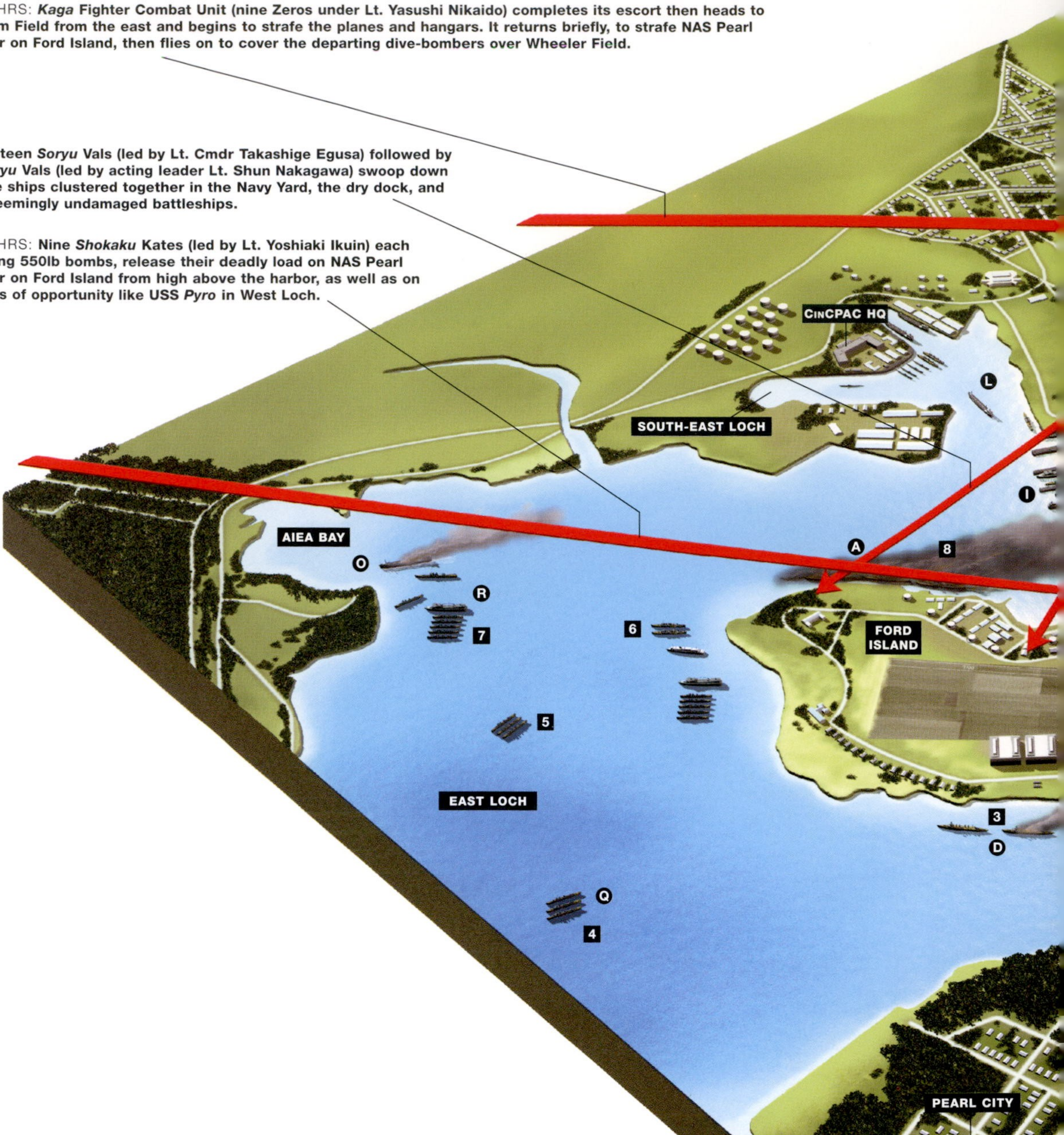

0902 HRS: *Kaga* Fighter Combat Unit (nine Zeros under Lt. Yasushi Nikaido) completes its escort then heads to Hickam Field from the east and begins to strafe the planes and hangars. It returns briefly, to strafe NAS Pearl Harbor on Ford Island, then flies on to cover the departing dive-bombers over Wheeler Field.

Seventeen *Soryu* Vals (led by Lt. Cmdr Takashige Egusa) followed by 17 *Hiryu* Vals (led by acting leader Lt. Shun Nakagawa) swoop down on the ships clustered together in the Navy Yard, the dry dock, and any seemingly undamaged battleships.

0902 HRS: Nine *Shokaku* Kates (led by Lt. Yoshiaki Ikuin) each carrying 550lb bombs, release their deadly load on NAS Pearl Harbor on Ford Island from high above the harbor, as well as on targets of opportunity like USS *Pyro* in West Loch.

CɪɴCPAC HQ

L

SOUTH-EAST LOCH

I

AIEA BAY

A   8

O

R   6

7   FORD ISLAND

5

EAST LOCH   3

D

Q

4

PEARL CITY

THE SECOND ATTACK WAVE PEARL HARBOR, 0905–0945 HRS

Tactically speaking, the Japanese attack was a success: few proposed targets were missed. *Arizona* and *Oklahoma* were so badly mauled that they would never return to service. A few ships did manage to get under way, but these were in the minority. Curiously, the fuel tank farms were not hit: the Japanese knew of them, but the ships were their chief targets, and burning fuel tanks would mask the ships. Just a few months later, the above-ground fuel tanks were replaced by below-ground fuel bunkers, the construction of which had begun before the war. Japanese losses during the Second Wave amounted to 20 aircraft, nine of them claimed by anti-aircraft fire.

0900 HRS: The Second Attack Wave arrives with a heavy punch. 2nd Attack Group (consisting of 78 Val dive-bombers, under Lt. Cmdr Takashige Egusa) arrives in the harbor from the northeast: the targets are Battleship Row, Ford Island and the Navy Yard, picking up any missed targets from the first wave.

Bomber attack formation:
Soryu 17 Vals (Lt. Cmdr Egusa)
Hiryu 17 Vals (Lt. Shun Nakagawa)
Akagi 18 Vals (Lt. Chihaya)
Kaga 26 Vals (Lt. Cmdr Makino)

Following the *Hiryu* Val unit, 18 Val dive-bombers in the *Akagi* unit (led by Lt. Takehiko Chihaya) target the tanker *Neosho* during her sortie, the floating dry dock, the northwest side of Ford Island, and the battleship *Maryland*.

Last to attack, three of the *Kaga* Val unit (led by Lt. Saburo Makino, 26 Val dive-bombers in total) continue the attack on *Maryland* and *West Virginia* when Makino diverts the rest to target *Nevada* during her sortie. The bombardment is intense.

HICKAM FIELD

NAVY YARD

TENTEN PIER

PEARL HARBOR NAS

G

H

C

F

9

K

P

N

WAIPIO POINT

HOSPITAL POINT

WEST LOCH

WAIPIO PENINSULA

B

E

M

BECKONING POINT

2

1

MIDDLE LOCH

N

KEY TO US SHIPS
(Refer to the map of the harbor on pages 28–29 for full details of US ship positions.)
1 *Ramsay, Gamble, Montgomery*
2 *Trever, Breese, Zane, Perry, Wasmuth, Medusa, Curtiss*
3 *Tangier, Utah, Raleigh, Detroit*
4 *Aylwin, Dale, Farragut*
5 *Ralph Talbot, Patterson, Henley*
6 *Phelps, MacDonough, Worden, Dewey, Hull, Dobbin, Solace, Allen, Chew*
7 *Phoenix, Blue, Whitney, Conyngham, Reid, Tucker, Case, Selfridge*
8 Battleship Row: *Vestal, Arizona, Tennessee, West Virginia, Maryland, Oklahoma, Neosho, California*
9 *Nevada*

KEY TO OVERALL US SHIP DAMAGE AND MOVEMENTS
A Battleship Row
   Oklahoma 9 torpedo hits: sunk.
   California 3 torpedo hits 0800–0810 hrs, 1 bomb hit 0910: listing.
   West Virginia 9 torpedo, 2 bomb hits: half-sunk.
   Arizona 2 bomb hits 0805 hrs, 0810 hrs: sunk.
   Maryland 2 bomb hits.
   Tennessee 2 bomb hits.
B *Utah* 2 torpedo hits: sunk.
C *Oglala* concussion (from torpedo hit on *Helena*) split seams, 0930 hrs: capsizes.
D *Raleigh* 1 torpedo hit 0755 hrs, 1 bomb hit 0912 hrs: listing.
E *Curtiss* Val crashes into her 0912 hrs, 1 bomb hit.
F *Shaw* 3 bomb hits 0910 hrs: badly damaged.
G *Pennsylvania* 1 bomb hit 0907 hrs.
H *Cassin* 1 bomb hit 0905 hrs.
   Downes 2 bomb hits 0905 hrs.
 I *Honolulu* bomb hits the dock wall 0909 hrs: buckled hull.
J *Helena* 1 torpedo hit 0757 hrs.
K *Nevada* 1 torpedo hit 0806 hrs, multiple bomb hits: beaches on Hospital Point.
L *Neosho* moves to Southeast Loch.
M *Monaghan* rams a Japanese midget sub at Middle Loch entrance.
N *St. Louis* moves south out of the harbor, fired on by a Japanese midget submarine just outside the harbor entrance but is not hit.
O *Vestal* 2 bomb hits: beaches on Aiea Sands 0945 hrs.
P *Helm* moves to the ocean 0820 hrs: encounters Japanese midget submarine.
Q *Alwyn* moves to the open sea, and exits the harbor at 0930 hrs.
R *Blue* moves to the open sea, and exits the harbor at 0940 hrs.

the 98th Coast Artillery, heard the engine drone of planes. He grabbed a Browning automatic rifle (BAR) and a couple of magazines and rushed outside. Sgt. Lowell Klatt did likewise and followed him. A radial-engined plane passed low overhead coming right at them. They stood their ground, opening up with the BARs, and both men emptied their magazines at the plane. It wobbled over the building, then lost altitude and crashed into Kapapa Gulch. The body of John Dains was found in the P-36 wreckage.

All over the island, radio stations urged civilians to get off the roads, go home, clear the streets, get under cover, declaring that this attack was "the Real McCoy." A bomb fell near Governor Poindexter's house, sending up a shower of earth and rattling doors and windows, and it turned out to be a naval artillery shell.

Lieutenant Commander W. Specht saw that all 12 of his PT boats were undamaged, both those at the sub base and those near *Ramapo*. His six functional torpedo boats got underway from the sub base and maneuvered around the debris in the harbor, patrolling, picking up wounded and drifting sailors and taking them to shore, where they were transferred to hospitals or returned to their ships.

At 1000 hrs, aircraft of the first wave returned to the task force and began landing on *Akagi*, *Kaga* and other carriers positioned 260 miles north of Oahu. Back on the island, Governor Poindexter issued a state of emergency for the entire Hawaiian territory, first to newspapers, and 15 minutes later via a radio broadcast. Reports of civilian casualties started coming in from hospitals, and by 1042 hrs all radio stations had shut off their transmitters to prevent them being used as homing beacons by attacking aircraft. Meanwhile, Gen. Short conferred with Poindexter about placing the entire territory under martial law while the first false reports of invading enemy troops began circulating. All schools were ordered closed. That night, and every night in the near future, there would be a blackout in Hawaii.

Surviving American aircraft took off from damaged fields and immediately began the search for their attackers. They flew 360 degrees, but did not sight the Japanese task force. At 1230 hrs, the Honolulu police, aided by the FBI, descended on the Japanese embassy, where they found consular personnel near wastepaper baskets full of ashes and still-burning documents.

Commander Fuchida touched down at 1300 hrs aboard the *Akagi*. He discussed launching a third wave with Adm. Nagumo, but Nagumo believed they had done well enough and decided not to launch another attack. At 1630 hrs, Nagumo turned the taskforce to withdraw.

Fuchikami delivered the message from Washington to Gen. Short's headquarters at 1145 hrs. It still had to be decoded and would not be seen by Short for another three hours. Almost seven hours after the attack had started, and easily seven and a half hours too late to be of any use, word of the now-past danger reached Short.

AFTERMATH

Japanese losses were minimal – negligible – in view of the victory they had won: 185 killed, one captured. American losses were staggering: 2,388 casualties (2,107 Navy/Marines, 233 Army, and 48 civilians) and 1,109 were wounded (710 Navy/Marines, 364 Army, and 35 civilians).

The *Arizona* saw the greatest loss of life, accounting for half the naval casualties. Losses included men from 44 states, the District of Columbia, Guam, Hawaii, the Philippines and Canada. As a result of Pearl Harbor, 16 Congressional Medals of Honor, 51 Navy Crosses, 53 Silver Crosses, four Navy and Marine Corps Medals, one Distinguished Flying Cross, four Distinguished Service Crosses, one Distinguished Service Medal, and three Bronze Stars were awarded for the 110 minutes of combat. A tally of vessels shows all eight battleships sunk or heavily damaged, testifying to the accuracy of Japanese attacks; three cruisers damaged; four destroyers damaged; one minelayer sunk; and two auxiliaries sunk or capsized and one heavily damaged. The US lost 169 aircraft (92 Navy and 77 Army) and 150 were damaged (31 Navy and 128 Army).

Japanese damage assessments
Fuchida flew over the harbor and recorded visible damage; once back aboard *Akagi*, he compared his notes with others' observations. Those

The devastation was immense: this shows a close-up of *Downes'* burnt hulk in dry dock; *Cassin* is capsized next to her. The superstructure in the background belongs to the battleship *Pennsylvania.*

aboard *Akagi* reported the high-level bombers had scored two hits on *Maryland* and one hit on *Tennessee*, and although the 3rd *Akagi* Squadron's success could not be verified because of cloud cover, they believed they, too, had inflicted one hit on *Tennessee*. Eleven torpedoes had struck home on three battleships. *Akagi* dive-bombers had not been able to assess accurately the damage to battleships because of smoke and fire, although one Omaha class cruiser (CL) was a known hit. *Akagi*'s fighters had shot down a B-17, a trainer and a transport, and of 40 aircraft on Hickam Field, 23 were ablaze while the remaining seven were seriously damaged. At Ewa, over 30 aircraft had been damaged or destroyed.

USS *Raleigh* was damaged during the attack. Shortly afterwards, pontoons were used to keep her upright so she could be repaired and refitted. *Utah*'s hull is capsized to the right of the tug.

Kaga's pilots reported eight torpedo hits on three battleships. High-level bombers damaged the aft of *Arizona*, put two hits on *West Virginia*, and one on *Tennessee*. Torpedo planes put hits on *West Virginia*, *Oklahoma*, and *Nevada*. Dive-bombers hit *West Virginia*, *Maryland* and had eight hits on *Nevada*. Two enemy aircraft had been shot down, one was damaged by strafing, and many of their target airfields were on fire after the mission.

Hiryu and *Soryu* reported six torpedo hits on a battleship with a cage mast (*Utah*), three hits on another battleship, which sank at once, two hits on yet another battleship, and one on a cruiser. Bombing had sunk one battleship (*Arizona*) instantaneously and hits had been observed on *Tennessee* and *West Virginia*. Clouds had interfered with all attacks, and two units missed *California* and *Nevada*. Dive-bombs had landed on *California*, *Pennsylvania*, *Maryland*, and *West Virginia*. Six hits were scored on heavy cruiser *Helena*. Dive-bombers put five hits on light cruisers and one on a docked destroyer, causing a mighty explosion. They had set 20 aircraft ablaze at Wheeler (including four light bombers and a flying boat) and destroyed four hangars; at Ewa, they had set 60 grounded aircraft ablaze, and at Kaneohe, ten.

Shokaku's and *Zuikaku*'s planes reported destroying two flying boat hangars and one for bombers at Ford Island. At Kaneohe, they had hit nearly 50 flying boats and their hangar, and they had burned 80 percent of the hangars at Wheeler Field and three aircraft at Bellows Field. At Hickam their attack had set seven hangars ablaze.

Confusion, because of multiple and overlapping attack responsibilities, had commanders duplicate results given by other commanders. Still, the message was clear. The attacks had been very successful.

RIGHT **Details of the damage inflicted on the *Nevada*.**

BELOW **The path through the harbor of the *Nevada*'s attempted escape.**

The real damage

Specific damage inflicted by the Japanese was staggering. Every battleship was badly damaged. Most major vessels had been shot up. Even detail reports of damage are conflicting because of the fog of war. One thing is certain: only the carriers that were absent were unscathed. Actual damage to the fleet and the subsequent fate of the ships was as follows:

US Ship Losses

Arizona BB39, two bomb hits, sunk; now a cemetery with memorial for those who died at Pearl Harbor.

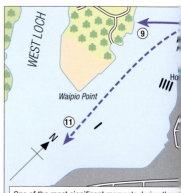

One of the most significant moments during the w[...] the attack on Pearl Harbor was the gallant sortie [...] of the USS *Nevada*. The sight of the ship moving [...] Battleship Row roused the morale of those who w[...] watching, in the US navy's darkest hours. The su[...] assault that she underwent during her break for f[...] resulted in the death of numerous crew members, in[...] Chief Boatswain Edwin J. Hill, who cast off *Nevada* [...] before swimming back to the ship.

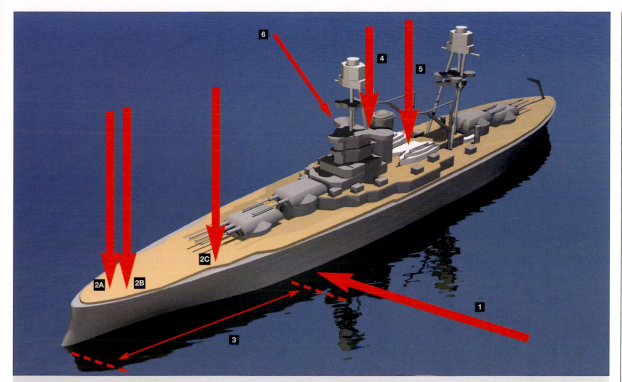

1 At 0805 hrs, a torpedo plane attacks *Nevada* while she is still berthed at the north-east end of Battleship Row. Gunners on board and neighboring ships manage to shoot it down aft of the ship, but the torpedo launched scores a hit on the port bow, at frame 40. The blast shakes the whole ship, and she begins to take on water. This constitutes the most significant damage done to *Nevada* during the whole of the Pearl Harbor attack.

2 0910 hrs, *Kaga* dive-bombers heading to hit ships on Battleship Row spot *Nevada* as she passes TenTen Pier in her break for safety, and swoop down on her from the south-west and south-east in a split formation (the idea is to confuse and split the American AA fire). Only the planes that attack "in the sun" manage to score hits with their bombs. The first eight planes, led by Lt.Cmdr Makino, and

the second squadron of nine Vals, led by Lt. Ogawa, target her foreturret and midsection. During this intense period of attack, she sustains three direct hits from Val dive-bombers in her fore (2A, 2B, and 2C). One of the Vals is hit in the engine and the plane sputters low across Ford Island, making a good target for gunners who chop the tail off as it crashes in Middle Loch. *Nevada* continues to take on water, but presses ahead.

3 Fire engulfs all the compartments on the second and main decks in the fore of the ship following the direct hits scored in this area. It will burn fiercely for 48 hours.

4 0915 hrs, the last *Kaga* unit of nine dive-bombers, under Lt. Ibuki, take over the attack. A fourth bomb hits the forecastle, causing considerable damage and costing the lives of several crew members.

5 A fifth bomb hits the *Nevada* shortly after, at the base of her rear tripod mast. Most of this last *Kaga* unit are hit heavily by AA fire, including one hit 22 times. One pilot is wounded yet is able to return to *Kaga*.

6 A powder fire has broken out in her gun casemate, to starboard of her rear tripod mast. The *Nevada* is by now sitting low in the water. Her acting captain realizes she is in danger of blocking the channel by sinking where she is, so the decision is taken to beach her near USS *Shaw*.

1. 0740 hrs: the *Nevada* is the last ship on Battleship Row, moored by herself. She has one boiler up and running, which enables her to get moving.
2. 0805 hrs, one *Kaga* torpedo plane launches toward her port bow while she is still at berth. Gunners on board and on the nearby *Chew* bring the plane down, but the torpedo hits at frame #40. She begins to take on water.
3. 0830 hrs, hi-level bombs splash off her port side, and Lt.Cmdr Francis J. Thomas (acting commander) decides to make a run for the sea – the damage done to the adjacent *Arizona* presses home the point. She reverses, then edges herself out at 0840 hrs, between the attack waves.
4. The *Nevada* is trailed throughout her sortie attempt by the tug boat *YT-153*: the tug was ordered to help her out of her berth, but found that *Nevada* had already gotten underway. The little tug follows her all the way down the channel, and is first on the scene when she eventually beaches.
5. 0842 hrs, the tanker *Neosho* reverses from her berth. A bit faster than *Nevada*, *Neosho* crosses in front of the battleship, heading for a berth in Southeast Loch. Neither has gotten far when the Second Wave arrives at 0902 hrs. Four dive-bombers target *Neosho* in her sortie.
6. As *Nevada* passes Ten Ten Pier at about 0910 hrs, the dive-bombers wake up to the importance of her sortie. *Kaga* units cut short their dives on Battleship Row and 23 Vals, led by Lt.Cmdr Makino, focus on *Nevada*.
7. *Nevada* negotiates her way past a dredge blocking part of the channel while sustaining five or more hits to her fore and mid-section. Blazing, the decision is taken to beach her, or else risk blocking the channel.
8. 0920 hrs. *Nevada* touches her bow on shore just west of the burning *Shaw*. The strong outbound current in the harbor's channel catches the *Nevada's* stern and swings her completely around, just as *Shaw* blows up at 0930 hrs.
9. After the attack *Nevada* is tugged stern first to Buoy 19 on Waipio Peninsula, where her bow sinks.
10. 0935 hrs, and *St. Louis* has also gotten underway in the confusion of the attack, slipping away from her berth in the repair basin of the Navy Yard.
11. USS *St. Louis* moves towards the open sea: later she is targeted by a Japanese midget submarine at the mouth of the channel, but escapes being hit by both of the torpedoes launched.

California BB44, three torpedo hits, one bomb hit, sunk; later raised.
Maryland BB46, two bomb hits, damaged; repaired and modernized.
Nevada BB36, one torpedo hit, five or more bomb hits, heavily
    damaged; run aground, repaired and modernized.
Oklahoma BB37, nine torpedo hits, capsized; raised and scrapped.
Pennsylvania BB38, one bomb hit, damaged; repaired.
Tennessee BB43, two bomb hits, damaged; repaired.
West Virginia BB48, two bomb hits, nine torpedo hits, sunk; raised,
    repaired and modernized.
Helena CL50, one torpedo hit, heavily damaged; repaired.
Honolulu CL48, one near bomb hit with collateral damage; repaired.
Raleigh CL7, one torpedo and one bomb hit, heavily damaged;
    repaired and refitted.
Cassin DD372, one bomb hit, one near miss, heavily damaged; rebuilt.
Downes DD375, one bomb hit, heavily damaged; rebuilt.
Helm DD388, one bomb near by, damaged; continued tour of duty,
    repaired on return.
Shaw DD373, three bomb hits, bow blown off in explosion; repaired.
Oglala CM4, concussion from nearby torpedo split seams, sunk; raised
    and repaired.
Curtiss AV4, one bomb hit, damaged; repaired.
Sotoyomo YT9, sunk; raised and repaired.
Utah AG16, two torpedo hits, capsized; now a cemetery.
Vestal AR4, two bomb hits, heavily damaged; grounded, refloated and
    repaired.
YFD-2 sunk; raised and repaired.

US Aircraft Losses
Bellows Field: two P-40s, one O-49, one B-17C.
Ewa Mooring Mast Field: 32 total including F4F, SBD and SB2U.
Ford Island: 26 total including PBY and J2F.
Hickam Field: two A-20s, 12 B-18s, four B-17Ds, one B-17C, one B-24A.
Kaneohe: 33 PBYs; one OS2U.
Wheeler Field: 30 P-40s; four P-36s; six P-26s; two OA-9s
USS Enterprise: six SBDs, including one to ground fire.

Japanese Losses
Aircraft: nine fighters, 15 dive-bombers, five torpedo planes.
Submarines: one I-class sub, five midget subs.
Casualties: 55 airmen, 121 submarine crewmen, nine midget sub
    crewmen.

    Before the oily smoke had drifted away, the United States was no
longer neutral. After two hours of air strikes, the day of the battleship
had passed as decisively as the day of horse cavalry. Air power, which had
been tolerated and given lip service by many, became the branch of
service of the hour.
    The United States would have entered World War II eventually, but
whether her entry would have been in time to aid Britain is open to
discussion. Certainly she would have butted heads with Japan sooner or
later. Had the great sea battle happened, many Japanese and American
vessels would have gone to the bottom where no one could have

The air attack left Wheeler Field in ruins. Here are the remains of aircraft hangars and shattered shells of airplanes, including a P-40 and a twin-engine amphibian.

recovered them, and the outcome of such a battle would have been inconclusive, for neither side was prepared for invasion. Had the American Navy waited and sortied, they would have lost carriers they could ill afford to lose much earlier than at Midway.

Yamamoto was correct in stating that the Japanese attack on Pearl Harbor awakened a sleeping giant, because it unified the American people (who were just recovering from the Depression) against a common enemy. While the atrocities and horrors of war occurred on European or Asian soil, Americans could ignore or lessen their impact, remaining officially uninvolved. Once American lives had been lost, they could no longer afford the luxury of neutrality or isolationism.

The Japanese were right to assume that the United States was the greatest threat to their growth in the Pacific, and Pearl Harbor put American response on the fast track. Payback was not long in coming, for the battle at Midway stopped the Japanese advance and curbed their naval superiority. Afterwards, the road to Tokyo took three long years and was paved with the steel and blood of both sides. Americans rallied around the icon of Pearl Harbor the way earlier generations had heeded the nationalistic imperative of "Remember the Alamo." The shame and anger they felt from the resounding defeat at Pearl Harbor could not be laid to rest until they had taken the war to Japanese soil.

In the gray days of fading sunlight of late December, 1941, the Americans turned their eyes to Europe and Asia, mouths grimly set, and tightened their belts for war production and conscription. Conditions would get worse before they could improve. Bataan, Wake, the Philippines, Midway, Coral Sea, the Solomons, and other names sent families to atlases to locate far-flung and exotic locations where loved ones flew, sailed, or slogged through jungle.

The war with Japan ended on the deck of the USS *Missouri* at 0903 hrs on September 2, 1945, in Tokyo Bay, but it all began at 0735 hrs, December 7, 1941, at Pearl Harbor.

USS ARIZONA

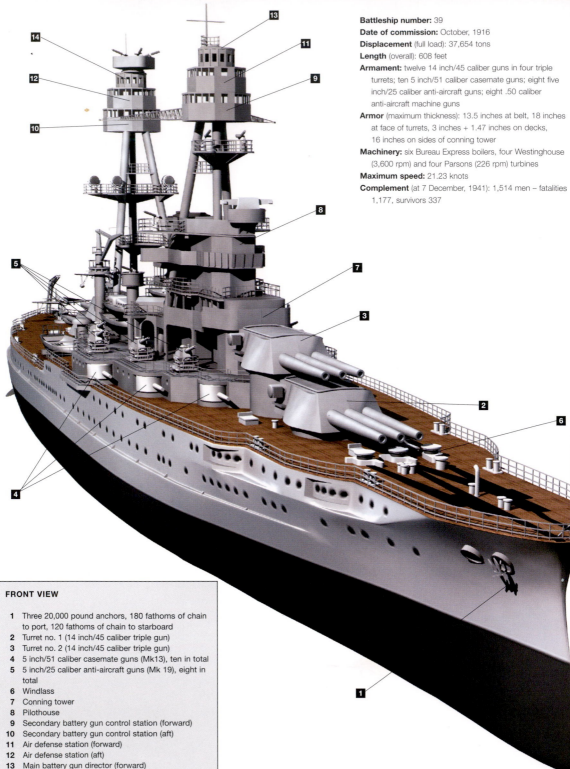

Battleship number: 39
Date of commission: October, 1916
Displacement (full load): 37,654 tons
Length (overall): 608 feet
Armament: twelve 14 inch/45 caliber guns in four triple turrets; ten 5 inch/51 caliber casemate guns; eight five inch/25 caliber anti-aircraft guns; eight .50 caliber anti-aircraft machine guns
Armor (maximum thickness): 13.5 inches at belt, 18 inches at face of turrets, 3 inches + 1.47 inches on decks, 16 inches on sides of conning tower
Machinery: six Bureau Express boilers, four Westinghouse (3,600 rpm) and four Parsons (226 rpm) turbines
Maximum speed: 21.23 knots
Complement (at 7 December, 1941): 1,514 men – fatalities 1,177, survivors 337

FRONT VIEW

1. Three 20,000 pound anchors, 180 fathoms of chain to port, 120 fathoms of chain to starboard
2. Turret no. 1 (14 inch/45 caliber triple gun)
3. Turret no. 2 (14 inch/45 caliber triple gun)
4. 5 inch/51 caliber casemate guns (Mk13), ten in total
5. 5 inch/25 caliber anti-aircraft guns (Mk 19), eight in total
6. Windlass
7. Conning tower
8. Pilothouse
9. Secondary battery gun control station (forward)
10. Secondary battery gun control station (aft)
11. Air defense station (forward)
12. Air defense station (aft)
13. Main battery gun director (forward)
14. Main battery gun director (aft)

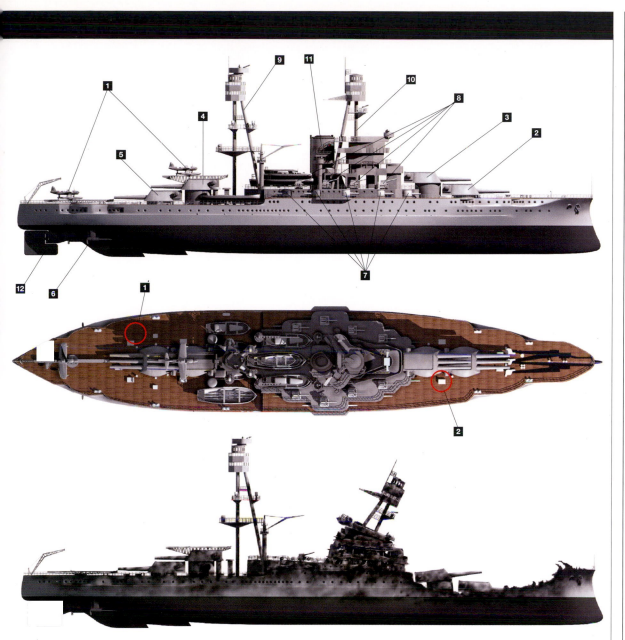

The damage inflicted

SIDE VIEW

1 Two OS2U Kingfisher planes, launch catapults and cranes
2 Turret no. 1 (14 inch/45 caliber triple gun)
3 Turret no. 2 (14 inch/45 caliber triple gun)
4 Turret no. 3 (14 inch/45 caliber triple gun)
5 Turret no. 4 (14 inch/45 caliber triple gun)
6 Four 12 feet 7 inch diameter propellers, each with three blades
7 5 inch/51 caliber casemate guns (Mk13), ten in total
8 5 inch/25 caliber anti-aircraft guns (Mk 19), eight in total
9 Tripod mainmast
10 Tripod foremast
11 Smokestack
12 Rudder

TOP VIEW

1 0805hrs, 800kg bomb hit
2 0806hrs, 800kg bomb hits the forward magazine, causing a massive explosion

RIGHT **In the background, the *Maryland*'s masts still fly the Stars and Stripes, while rescuers work on the hull of the capsized *Oklahoma* to free trapped crewmen.**

ABOVE LEFT **The view from the heavily damaged Consolidated Barracks towards Hickam Field's flight line. Engines from Captain Ray Swenson's B-17C (center of picure) have been salvaged. To the left and in front of the B-17 sits an obsolete A-12 "Shrike".**

BELOW LEFT **Just visible to the left of the picture, tugs latch onto the wreckage of a B-18 bomber on the ramp at Hickam Field.**

BELOW RIGHT **Although the Japanese suffered few casualties, not all pilots made it home safely. This Zero was shot down during the attack.**

BOTTOM LEFT **Schofield Barracks stood three stories tall and was a strafing target of the Japanese. Surrounded by parade grounds, Schofield was easy for attackers to target. Schofield shot down one plane, an American P-36 trying to land at neighboring Wheeler Field.**

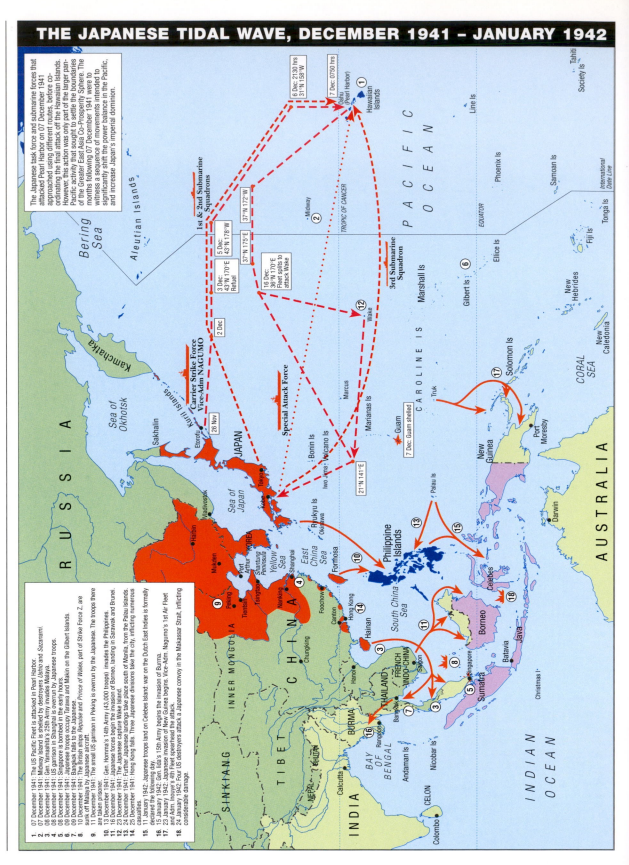

PEARL HARBOR TODAY

The bright sun reflects dazzlingly from blue waters surrounding the walkway, strong enough to give you a headache if you are not wearing sunglasses. Sound carries a great distance over water, and the roar of planes landing at the nearby international airport draws to mind the events which pulled the United States into World War II. All is peaceful, as Cmdr Fuchida noted over half a century ago. Today the American flag undulates on the sea breeze above the sunken remains of the USS *Arizona*. Contrary to urban legend, *Arizona* is not carried on the in-service roll.

How to get there

If you don't want any hassle, consider taking a tour bus. Ask your hotel concierge or use the yellow pages to find the phone numbers of tour bus companies and call for scheduled Pearl Harbor tours.

Visitors to Oahu can either take the bus or rent a car to visit the site. Buses leave from several locations around Waikiki and offer a regular scheduled service. The No. 20 bus is the best bet, as it offers a direct service, but the No. 47 bus also goes there. If in doubt, ask the hotel concierge for a bus route, a map, and advice on which bus to catch, where to transfer and so on. Other buses go past the Memorial bus stop at the Ala Moana shopping center. For schedules or details, call (808) 848 5555, the bus information number.

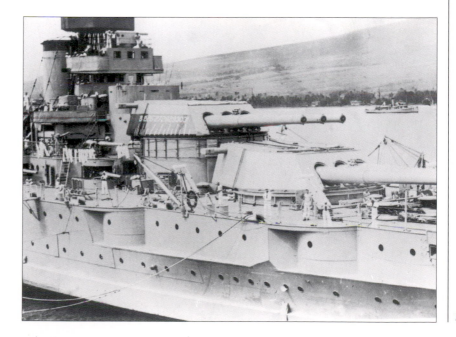

Pennsylvania was in dry dock, and because she was somewhat protected from both aerial and torpedo attacks, damage was less than on other battleships. This picture, taken several years earlier, shows her six forward guns. Note the hospital ship and tug in the background off her port side.

By car, take Kalia Road east. Go through Ft. De Russey to Ala Moana Boulevard. Turn left onto Ala Moana Boulevard and follow it past the Ala Moana shopping center. Once past the shopping center, this road merges with Nimitz Highway (Highway 92) and changes to that name. Stay on Nimitz past all the Honolulu airport exits until you reach Kamehameha Highway (Highway 99), which is past the airport. Bear right to enter Kamehameha Highway. Follow it past the Navy Halawa Gate and housing area. You will see signs for the Pearl Harbor Visitor Center, which is on your left, and visitor parking is available.

The Visitor Center

The Visitor Center was dedicated in 1962 and became a part of the National Park Service system in 1980. Over one-and-a-half million visitors come through this park each year. As Hawaii is a tropical island, wear sunscreen and light clothing, and take a light waterproof jacket or umbrella for afternoon showers.

The USS Arizona Visitor Center lies within the Pearl Harbor Naval Base and is a monument now operated and maintained by the National Park Service through an arrangement with the United States Navy. The park consists of a visitor center, theater, museum, bookshop and waterfront exhibits. Nearby is the USS *Bowfin* submarine exhibit and park. The Arizona Monument floats above the sunken remains of the USS *Arizona* and the honored seamen who rest within her rusting bosom. A flag is raised and lowered over the memorial each day.

As a National Park Service site, the Arizona Memorial is open daily from 0730 hrs to 1700 hrs year round except on special holidays (Thanksgiving, Christmas Day, and New Year's Day). Special programs run on December 7, and Memorial Day. Although admission is free, donations to help defray costs of upkeep are encouraged.

Tourists arriving at the center are issued tickets. This is to ensure that everyone who wants to see the memorial can do so in an orderly manner. Tours are on a first come, first served basis – you cannot make reservations. At the center, a 23-minute film produced by the National

After the attack, Nagumo decided the Japanese had done well enough. The US feverishly labored to raise sunken ships. From top left to bottom right, the vessels are *California*, *Maryland* (afloat), *Oklahoma* (capsized), *Tennessee*, *West Virginia*, and *Arizona*. The oil slick is primarily from *Arizona*.

Park Service gives visitors an overview of the history and events leading up to the Japanese attack on the US warships at Pearl Harbor. After viewing the film, visitors catch a shuttle boat out to the memorial. The total program takes about one hour and 15 minutes. Tours begin at 0800 hrs. There is usually a short wait because the memorial is one of the best-known tourist meccas in Hawaii, and waits of up to an hour are not uncommon. It is usually best to schedule this as the first event of the day because of this. The last program of the day begins at 1500 hrs.

Information
The monument address: USS Arizona Memorial, 1 Arizona Memorial Place, Honolulu, HA 96818-3145, telephone (808) 422 2771 or (808) 422 0561 for recorded messages.

Take your camera, sunscreen and plenty of film to record the quiet, seaborne tranquillity of one of Oahu's most-visited historic locations.

FURTHER READING

Agawa, Hiroyuki (trans. John Bester), *The Reluctant Admiral: Yamamoto and the Imperial Navy*, Kodansha International Ltd., Tokyo, 1979

Albright, Harry, *Pearl Harbor: Japan's Fatal Blunder*, Hippocrene Books, New York, NY, 1988

Arroyo, Ernest, *Pearl Harbor*, Metrobooks, New York, 2001

Bagnasco, Ermino, *Submarines of World War II*, Naval Institute Press, Annapolis, MD, 1977

Barker, A. J., Col. (retired), *Pearl Harbor: Tora, Tora, Tora*, Ballantine Books, New York, NY, 1988

Boatner, Mark M., III, *The Biographical Dictionary of World War II*, Presidio Press, Novato, CA, 1996

Breuer, William, *Devil Boats: The PT War Against Japan*, Presidio Press, Novato, CA, 1987

Carpenter, Dorr, and Polmar, Norman, *Submarines of the Imperial Japanese Navy*, Naval Institute Press, Annapolis, MD, 1996

Clausen, Henry C., and Bruce, Lee, *Pearl Harbor: Final Judgment*, Crown Publishers, New York, NY, 1992

Cohen, Stan, *Attack on Pearl Harbor*, MT: Pictorial Histories, Missoula, 2001

Devereaux, James P. S., *The Story of Wake Island*, J.P. Lippincott Co., New York, NY, 1947

Dull, Paul S., *A Battle History of the Imperial Japanese Navy (1941–1945)*, Naval Institute Press, Annapolis, MD, 1978

Dyer, V-Adm George C., *On the Treadmill to Pearl Harbor: The Memoirs of Admiral James O. Richardson, USN (Retired)*, Naval History Division, Washington DC, 1973

Editors of Army Times, *A Military History: Pearl Harbor and Hawaii*, Bonanza Books, New York, NY, 1971

Esposito, Vincent J., Col. USA, *The West Point Atlas of American Wars, Vol. I*, Frederick A. Praeger Publishers, New York, NY, 1959

Fahey, James C., *The Ships and Aircraft of the US Fleet (Fahey's Second War Edition)*, Gemsc Inc., New York, NY, 1944

Farago, Ladislas, *The Broken Seal*, Random House, New York, 1967

Fukodome, Shigeru, V/Adm. IJN (retired), *Hawaii Operation*, United States Naval Institute Proceedings, Annapolis, MD, 1955

Goldstein, Donald M., and Dillon, Katherine V., *The Pearl Harbor Papers: Inside The Japanese Plans*, Brassey's US, Mclean, VA, 1993

Green, William, and Swanborough, Gordon, *The Complete Book of Fighters*, Smithmark Books, New York, NY, 1994

Hara, Tameichi, Cpt. IJN (retired), Saito, Fred, and Pineau, Roger, *Japanese Destroyer Captain*, Ballantine Books, New York, NY, 1961

Hata, Ikuhiko, and Izawa, Yasuho (trans. D. C. Gorham), *Japanese Naval Aces and Fighter Units in World War II*, Naval Institute Press, Annapolis, MD, 1989

Heinrichs, Waldo H., *Threshold of war: Franklin D. Roosevelt and American entry into World War II*, Oxford University Press, New York, 1988

Hoyt, Edwin P., *The Last Kamikaze: the Story of Admiral Matome Ugaki*, Praeger Publishers, Westport, CT, 1993

Ienaga, Saburo (trans. Frank Baldwin), *The Pacific War 1931–1945*, Pantheon Books, New York, NY, 1978

Jane's Fighting Ships of World War II, Crescent Books, Avenel, NJ, 1995 (reprint)

Kahn, David, *The Codebreakers*, Macmillan, New York, 1967

Keegan, John, *The Second World War*, Penguin Books, New York, NY, 1990

Kennedy, John S., *The Forgotten Warriors of Kaneohe*, East Bay Blue Print, Oakland, CA, 1996 [Contact John S. Kennedy, 17271 Via Carmen, San Lorenzo, CA 94580-2611, USA, e-mail: siddorken@aol.com, for all enquiries]

LaForte, Robert S., and Marcello, Ronald E., *Remembering Pearl Harbor: Eyewitness Accounts by US Military Men and Women*, SR Books, Wilmington, DE, 1991

Layton, Edwin T., *"And I was there": Pearl Harbor and Midway – breaking the secrets*, William Morrow, New York, 1985

Lord, Walter, *Day of Infamy*, Bantam Books, New York, NY, 1963

McCombs, Don, and Worth, Fred L., *World War II: Strange & Fascinating Facts*, Greenwich House, New York, NY, 1983

McIntyre, Donald, Cpt. (retired), *Aircraft Carrier: The Majestic Weapon*, Ballantine Books, New York, NY, 1971

Miller, Edward S., *War Plan Orange: the U.S. strategy to defeat Japan, 1897-1945*, Naval Institute Press, Annapolis, 1991

Morisson, Samuel Eliot, Adm. USN (retired), *The Two Ocean War*, Ballantine Books, New York, NY, 1963

Morrison, Wilbur H., *Above and Beyond 1941–1945*, Bantam Books, New York, NY, 1983

Prados, John, *Combined Fleet Decoded: the secret history of American intelligence and the Japanese Navy in World War II*, Random House, New York, 1995

Prange, Gordon W., Goldstein, Donald M., and Dillon, Katherine V., *At Dawn We Slept: The Untold Story of Pearl Harbor*, Penguin Books USA Inc., New York, NY, 1982

Prange, Gordon W., Goldstein, Donald M., and Dillon, Katherine V., *Pearl Harbor: The Verdict of History*, Penguin Books USA Inc., New York, NY, 1986

Prange, Gordon W., Goldstein, Donald M., and Dillon, Katherine V., *Dec. 7 1941: The Day the Japanese Attacked Pearl Harbor*, Warner Books, New York, NY, 1988

Reilly, John C., Jr, *United States Navy Destroyers of World War II*, Blandford Press, Poole, Dorset, 1983

Rodriggs, Lawrence R., *We Remember Pearl Harbor: Honolulu civilians recall the war years, 1941-1945*, Communications Concepts, Newark, California, 1991

Smith, S. E. (Ed.), *The United States Navy in World War II*, Quill Books, William Morrow, New York, NY, 1966

Smurthwaite, David, *The Pacific War Atlas: 1941–1945*, Facts on File, New York, NY, 1995

Toland, John, *But Not In Shame*, Ballantine Books, New York, NY, 1961
    Infamy: Pearl Harbor and its Aftermath, Berkeley Publishing, New York, NY, 1983
    The Rising Sun: The Decline and Fall of the Japanese Empire, 1936-1945, Random House, New York, 1970

Wallin, Homer N., V/Adm., *Pearl Harbor: Why, How, Fleet Salvage and Final Appraisal*, US Government Printing Office, Naval History Division, Washington, DC, 1968

Watts, Anthony J., *Japanese Warships of World War II*, Doubleday & Co., Garden City, NY, 1966

Weintraub, Stanley, *Long Days Journey into War: December 7, 1941*, Truman Talley Books, New York, NY, 1991

Wels, Susan, *December 7, 1941: Pearl Harbor, America's Darkest Day*, Tehabi Books, San Diego, 2001

Wohlstetter, Roberta, *Pearl Harbor, Warning and Decision*, Stanford University Press, Stanford, 1962

Young, Peter, Brig. (retired) (Ed.), *The World Almanac Book of World War II*, Bison Books Ltd, London, 1981

Zacharias, R-Adm Ellis M., *Secret Missions: The Story of an Intelligence Officer*, G.P. Putnam's Sons, New York, 1946

Zich, Arthur, *World War II: The Rising Sun*, Time-Life Books, Alexandria, VA, 1977

APPENDICES

JAPANESE FIRST WAVE ATTACK FORMATION

Group, carrier of origin, and unit	Aircraft types	Armament	Mission	Division commander	Overall commander
FIRST GROUP					
1st Attack Unit *Akagi* (Aircraft tail ID: AI-)	5 Kates 5 Kates 5 Kates	800kg AP bomb	*Maryland* *Tennessee, West Virginia* *Tennessee, West Virginia*	**1st** Lt.Cmdr Mitsuo Fuchida **2nd** Lt. Goro Iwasaki **3rd** Lt. Izumi Furukawa	Lt.Cmdr Mitsuo Fuchida (AI-301)
2nd Attack Unit *Kaga* (Aircraft tail ID: AII-)	5 Kates 5 Kates 4 Kates	800kg AP bomb	*Tennessee, West Virginia* *Arizona/Vestal* *Tennessee, West Virginia*	**1st** Lt.Cmdr Takahashi Hashiguchi **2nd** Lt. Hideo Maki **3rd** Lt. Yoshitaka Mikami	Lt.Cmdr Takahashi Hashiguchi (AII-201)
3rd Attack Unit *Soryu* (Aircraft tail ID: BI-)	5 Kates 5 Kates	800kg AP bomb	*Tennessee, West Virginia* *Nevada*	**1st** Lt. Heijiro Abe **2nd** Lt. Sadao Yamamoto	Lt. Heijiro Abe
4th Attack Unit *Hiryu* (Aircraft tail ID: BII-)	5 Kates 5 Kates	800kg AP bomb	*Arizona, Vestal* *California*	**1st** Lt.Cmdr Tadashi Kusumi **2nd** Lt. Toshio Hashimoto	Lt.Cmdr Tadashi Kusumi
1st Torpedo Attack Unit *Akagi*	6 Kates 6 Kates	Mk 91 aerial torpedo	*West Virginia, Oklahoma* *California, West Virginia or Oklahoma*	**4th** Lt.Cmdr Shigeharu Murata **5th** Lt. Asao Negishi	Lt.Cmdr Shigeharu Murata (AI-311)
2nd Torpedo Attack Unit *Kaga*	6 Kates 6 Kates	Mk 91 aerial torpedo	*West Virginia, Oklahoma* *West Virginia, Nevada, or Oklahoma*	**1st** Lt. Kazuyoshi Kitajima **2nd** Lt. Mimori Suzuki	Lt. Kazuyoshi Kitajima (AII-311)
3rd Torpedo Attack Unit *Soryu*	4 Kates 4 Kates	Mk 91 aerial torpedo	*California, Utah, Helena* *Raleigh, Utah*	**1st** Lt. Tsuyoshi Nagai **2nd** Lt. Tatsumi Nakajima	Lt. Tsuyoshi Nagai (BI-311)
4th Torpedo Attack Unit *Hiryu*	4 Kates 4 Kates	Mk 91 aerial torpedo	*West Virginia, Oklahoma* *Helena*	**1st** Lt. Hirata Matsumura **2nd** Lt. Hiruharo Sumino	Lt. Hirata Matsumura (BII-320)
SECOND GROUP					
15th Attack Unit *Shokaku* (Aircraft tail ID: EI-)	9 Vals 8 Vals 9 Vals	250kg general purpose dive-bomb	NAS Pearl Harbor Hickam Field Hickam Field	**1st** Lt.Cmdr Kakuichi Takahashi **2nd** Lt. Masao Yamaguchi **3rd** Lt. Hisayoshi Fujita	Lt. Cmdr Kakuichi Takahashi (EI-238)
16th Attack Unit *Zuikaku* (Aircraft tail ID: EII-)	9 Vals 6 Vals (est.) 10 Vals (est.)	250kg general purpose dive-bomb	Wheeler Field Wheeler Field Wheeler Field	**1st** Lt. Akira Sakamoto **2nd** Lt. Tomatsu Ema **3rd** Lt. Hayashi	Lt. Akira Sakamoto (EII-201)
THIRD GROUP					
1st Fighter Combat Unit *Akagi*	9 Zeros	20mm cannon and 7.7mm MG	Hickam Field and Ewa Air control and strafing grounded aircraft at Ewa and Hickam Field	**2nd** Lt.Cmdr Shigeru Itaya	Lt.Cmdr Shigeru Itaya (AI-155)
2nd Fighter Combat Unit *Kaga*	9 Zeros	20mm cannon and 7.7mm MG	Hickam Field Air control and strafing grounded aircraft at Hickam Field and Ewa	**1st** Lt. Yoshio Shiga	Lt. Yoshio Shiga (AII-105)
3rd Fighter Combat Unit *Soryu*	8 Zeros	20mm cannon and 7.7mm MG	Wheeler Field and Ewa Air control and strafing grounded aircraft at Wheeler Field and Ewa	**3rd** Lt. Masaji Suganami	Lt. Masaji Suganami
4th Fighter Combat Unit *Hiryu*	6 Zeros	20mm cannon and 7.7mm MG	Ewa Air Control and strafing grounded aircraft at Ewa	**4th** Lt. Kiyoguma Okajima	Lt. Kiyoguma Okajima (BII-101)
5th Fighter Combat Unit *Shokaku*	6 Zeros	20mm cannon	NAS Kaneohe and Bellows Field. Air control and strafing grounded aircraft at Kaneohe	**5th** Lt. Tadashi Kaneko	Lt. Tadashi Kaneko (EI-101)
6th Fighter Combat Unit *Zuikaku*	5 Zeros	20mm cannon and 7.7mm MG	NAS Kaneohe Air control and strafing grounded aircraft at Kaneohe	**6th** Lt. Masao Sato	Lt. Masao Sato (EII-137)

JAPANESE SECOND WAVE ATTACK FORMATION

Group, carrier of origin, and unit	Aircraft types	Armament	Mission	Division commander	Overall commander
FIRST GROUP					Lt.Cmdr Shigekazu Shimazaki
5th Attack Unit *Shokaku* Aircraft tail ID EI-	9 Kates 9 Kates 9 Kates	1 x 250kg general purpose bomb and 6 x 60kg regular bombs, or 2 x 250kg bombs for high altitude bombing	Kaneohe NAS Kaneohe NAS Pearl Harbor NAS	**1st** Lt. Tatsuo Ichihara **2nd** Lt. Tsutomu Hagiwara **3rd** Lt. Yoshiaki Ikuin	Lt. Tatsuo Ichihara
6th Attack Unit *Zuikaku* Aircraft tail ID EII-	9 Kates 9 Kates 9 Kates	1 x 250kg general purpose bomb and 6 x 60kg regular bombs, or 2 x 250kg bombs for high altitude bombing	Hickam Field Hickam Field Hickam Field	**1st** Lt.Cmdr Shigekazu Shimazaki **2nd** Lt. Jyozo Iwami **3rd** Lt. Yoshiaki Tsubota	Lt.Cmdr Shigekazu Shimazaki
SECOND GROUP					Lt.Cmdr Takashige Egusa
11th Attack Unit *Soryu* Aircraft tail ID BI-	9 Vals 8 Vals	250kg general purpose dive-bomb	Navy Yard, *California* Navy Yard, *California, Dobbin, Pennsylvania*	**1st** Lt.Cmdr Takashige Egusa **2nd** Lt. Masai Ikeda	Lt.Cmdr Takashige Egusa (BI-231)
12th Attack Unit *Hiryu* Aircraft tail ID BII-	8 Vals 9 Vals	250kg general purpose dive-bomb	*California, Helena* and *Maryland* *Helm, Rigel*	**1st** Lt. Michio Kobayashi **2nd** Lt. Shun Nakagawa	Lt. Michio Kobayashi (unable to fly due to engine trouble) Lt. Shun Nakagawa, acting c.o.
13th Attack Unit *Akagi* Aircraft tail ID AI-	9 Vals 9 Vals	250kg general purpose dive-bomb	Ford Island NW, *Neosho, Shaw Raleigh, Maryland*	**1st** Lt. Takehiko Chihaya **2nd** Lt. Zenji Abe	Lt.Takehiko Chihaya
14th Attack Unit *Kaga* Aircraft tail ID AII-	8 Vals 9 Vals 9 Vals	250kg general purpose dive-bomb	*Nevada* *Maryland, West Virginia, Nevada* *Nevada*	**1st** Lt.Cmdr Saburo Makino **2nd** Lt. Shoichi Ogawa **3rd** Lt. Shoichi Ibuki	Lt.Cmdr Saburo Makino (AII-250)
THIRD GROUP					Lt. Saburo Shindo
1st Fighter Combat Unit *Akagi* Aircraft tail ID AI-	9 Zeros	20mm cannon and 7.7mm MG	Hickam Field	**1st** Lt. Saburo Shindo	Lt. Saburo Shindo (AI-201)
2nd Fighter Combat Unit *Kaga* Aircraft tail ID AII-	9 Zeros	20mm cannon and 7.7mm MG	Hickam Field, Pearl Harbor NAS, Wheeler	**2nd** Lt. Yasushi Nikaido	Lt. Yasushi Nikaido (AII-121)
3rd Fighter Combat Unit *Soryu* Aircraft tail ID BI-	9 Zeros	20mm cannon and 7.7mm MG	NAS Kaneohe	**3rd** Lt. Fusata Iida	Lt. Fusata Iida
4th Fighter Combat Unit *Hiryu* Aircraft tail ID BII-	9 Zeros	20mm cannon and 7.7mm MG	NAS Kaneohe and Bellows Field	**4th** Lt. Sumio Nono	Lt. Sumio Nono

BELOW **After the attack, all troops were put on alert, and artillery deployed in prepared positions, as shown here. Rumor had it that invasion was at hand. However, the invasion never materialized.**

JAPANESE ORGANIZATION

Prime Minister
Gen. Hideki Tojo

Japanese Combined Fleet Commander-in-Chief
Adm. Isoroku Yamamoto

1st Air Fleet C-in-C / Commander Hawaii Operation
V.Adm. Chuichi Nagumo

1st Carrier Div.	2nd Carrier Div.	5th Carrier Div.
Akagi , Kaga	*Soryu, Hiryu*	*Shokaku, Zuikaku*

1st Destroyer Sqdn Commander: R.Adm. Sentaro Omori	3rd Battleship Div. Commander: V.Adm. Gunichi Mikawa	2nd Submarine Div.Commander: Cpt. Kijiro Imaizumi	7th Destroyer Div. Commander: Cpt. Kaname Ohishi
1st Destroyer Sqdn *Abukuma* 17th Destroyer Sqdn *Tanikaze, Urakaze, Isokaze, Hamakaze*	**3rd BB Div.** *Hiei, Kirishima*	**2nd Sub. Div.** *I-19, I-21, I-23*	**7th Destroyer Div.** *Akebono, Ushio*

1st Supply Train
Cpt. Masanao Oto
Kyokuto Maru, Kenyo Maru, Kokuyo Maru, Shinkoku Maru

2nd Supply Train
Cpt. Kazutaka
Niimi Toei Maru, Toho Maru, Nihon Maru

Units working in conjunction with Hawaii Operation

Sixth Submarine Fleet
V.Adm. Mitsumi Shimizu (*Katori,* flagship of 6th SS fleet)

1st Squadron R.Adm. Tsutomu Sato *I-9, I-15, I-17, I-25* Mission: raid and blockade Oahu	2nd Squadron R.Adm. Shigeaki Yazazaki *I-1, I-2, I-3, I-4, I-5, I-6, I-7* Mission: raid and blockade Oahu	3rd Squadron R.Adm. Shigeoshi Miwa *I-8, I-68, I-69, I-70, I-71, I-72, I-73, I-74, I-75* Mission: raid and blockade Oahu
Special Attack Unit Cpt. Hanku Sasaki *I-16, I-18, I-20, I-22, I-24* Special Attack Unit submarines all carried midget 2-man submarines	**Recon** Cmdr Yasuchika Kashihara *I-10, I-26* Mission: intelligence gathering and recon	

US ORGANIZATION
7 December 1941

War Department
Secretary of War: Henry L. Stimson

Chief of Staff
Gen. Geo. C. Marshall

DCS / General Admin. and Ground Forces Maj.Gen. W. Bryden	DCS / Army Forces and Supply Maj.Gen. R.C. Moore	DCS / Air Maj.Gen. H.H. Arnold

G-1 Personnel	G-2 Intelligence Brig.Gen. Sherman Miles	G-3 Operations and Training	G-4 Supply Adjutant	The Judge Advocate General
	Counter Intelligence Lt.Col. J. T. Bissell	War Plans Division Brig.Gen. L.T. Gerow	Chief Signal Officer Maj.Gen. D. Olmstead	
	Intelligence Col. H.A. Kroner		Operations Col. O.K. Sadtler	
	Far Eastern Section Col. R.S. Bratton		Traffic and Signal Center Col. E.T. French	
	Japan Lt.Col. C.C. Dusenbury, 2nd-Lt. J.B. Schinde		Signal Intelligence Service Col. R.W. Minckler	
			Principal Cryptanalyst W.F. Friedman	

Navy Department

Secretary of the Navy
Frank Knox

Chief of Naval Operations
Adm. H.R. Stark

CinCPAC
Adm. H. Kimmel

Commandant 14th Naval District
Commander Hawaiian Naval Coastal Frontier
Pearl Harbor Navy Yard
R.Adm. R.C. Bloch (Commander Task Force Four)

Chief of Staff
Cpt. J.B. Earle

Intelligence Officer Cpt. I.H. Mayfield	Communications Security-Intelligence Cmdr J.J. Rochefort

Commander Naval Base Defense Air Force Commander Task Force Nine Commander Hawaiian Patrol Wing and Patrol Wing Two
R.Adm. P.N.L. Bellinger

LEFT After Pearl Harbor, the Japanese reconstructed the harbor and Battleship Row to how it was just prior to the attack – for use in a motion picture. Rear Admiral Shafroth gave this photo, captured after the war, to Adm. Nimitz.

Hawaiian Army Command

Commanding officer			
Lt.Gen. Walter C. Short			
Chief of Staff			
Col. W.C. Phillips			
G-1 Personnel	**G-2 Intelligence**	**G-3 Operations and Training**	**G-4 Supply**
Lt.Col. R.C. Throck-morton	Lt.Col. K.J. Fiedler	Lt.Col. W.E. Donegan	Col. M.W. Marston
Adjutant General Col. R.H. Dunlop		**24th Inf. Division** Brig.Gen. D.S. Wilson	
		25th Inf. Division Maj.Gen. Maxwell Murray	
Signal Corps Lt.Col. C.A. Powell			
		Coast Artillery Command Maj.Gen. H.T. Burgen	

Hawaiian Army Air Force

Hawaiian Department	
Lt. Gen. Walter C. Short	
Commanding officer	
Maj.Gen. Frederick L. Martin	
Chief of Staff	
Col. J.A. Mollison	
Intelligence Col. E.W. Bailey	**18th Bombardment Wing** Brig.Gen. J.H. Rudolph
	14th Pursuit Wing Brig.Gen. H.C. Davidson
Signal Officer Lt.Col. C.I. Hoppaugh	**Hickam Field** Col. W.E. Farthing
	Wheeler Field Col. W.J. Flood
	Bellows Field Lt.Col. L.D. Weddington

US Pacific Fleet

Commander in Chief Pacific Fleet (CinCPAC)					
Adm. H.E. Kimmel					
Chief of Staff					
Cpt. W.E. Smith					
Operations Officer Cpt. W.S. Delany	**War Plans Officer** Cpt. C.E. McMorris	**Gunnery Officer** Cmdr W.A. Kitts	**Communications Officer** Cmdr M.E. Curts	**Aviation Officer** Cmdr A. Davis	**Intelligence Officer** Lt.Cmdr E.T. Layton
1st Asst. Ops Officer Cmdr R.F. Good					**Task Force 1** V.Adm. W.S. Pye
					Task Force 2 V.Adm. W.F. Halsey
					Task Force 3 V.Adm. W. Brown
					Task Force 4 R.Adm. C.C. Bloch
					Task Force 7 R.Adm. T. Withers
					Task Force 9 R.Adm. P.N.L. Bellinger
					Task Force 15 R.Adm. W.L. Calhoun

LEFT **In prewar Hawaii, soldiers led a routine life. Many on guard duty walked their tour in Class As with highly polished brass, white gloves, and chin straps instead of fatigues. On December 7, 1941, this changed.**

BELOW **Although capable of absorbing vast amounts of damage, grounded B-17s fared no better than any other aircraft on the landing strip when faced with Japanese direct hits. This B-17 at Hickam's Hangar 5 shows the aftermath and destruction of the Japanese thrust.**

INDEX

Sunset at Schofield Barracks. The military waited for the other shoe to drop but, contrary to military expectations, there was no follow-up attack, even though the US was now at war.